My Life of Violence
(A TRUE STORY)
Barn Hole Publishing / Published by arrangement with
the author

Barn Hole Publishing first edition
Published 2016

Published by Barn Hole Publishing
Port Saint Lucie, FL
Printed on demand by Create space of Amazon Books

A WORD OF EXPLANATION BY THE
AUTHOR:

This is a true story of one woman's life
with violence. I wrote this to help with my own
healing. Writing this book has been a form of
therapy for me and perhaps better than professional
therapy might have been.

Being in a dysfunctional relationship for so
long, battling extreme violence has been baffling
until now. Seeing the relationship now from the
outside has revealed its true nature.

I've heard of an analogy about only being
able to see the room that you are in and, not being
able to see the house until outside of it.

Cover design by Barn Hole Publishing

ISBN 1532977344

My Life of Violence

(A TRUE STORY)

By: Shelby Snow

This book is dedicated to my sons, my friends Donnetta, Sandra and my nieces: Tiff, Sam, Tasha, Candy, Vanna and Katrina. I love you all so much.

Contents

Chapter 1

Meeting Jack

My story started when I was 17 years old. Moved out of my parent's house, and decided I wanted to go out and brave the world on my own. I rented a room in a boarding house and thought life was great.

I went back to school to get my GED because I dropped out of school in the beginning of the 11th grade, and needing to get a job was on my agenda.

I picked up a babysitting job to make some extra money; my life changed forever. I was babysitting for a lady full time 50 hours a week and, things were looking good.

One day I was babysitting when downstairs on the first floor porch I heard screaming while both babies were sleeping. I went outside the door to see what was going on. There was the new guy from New York screaming at a girl to get out and repeatedly calling her names. At that point I yelled down and asked. "Could you please keep from screaming, I am watching 2 small children who are sleeping." He turned around and said, "I'm very sorry and it wouldn't happen again." He then proceeded to ask my name. I said, "I'm Shelby." He said, "My name is Jack, I just moved up from Queens, New York." I said, "Well I got to go, nice to meet you." From that moment on he became obsessed with me. Every time I babysat which was everyday he was waiting for me. He knew when I left work and, he kept begging me to just have coffee with him, so finally I said, "Alright I will come over for coffee." So I did. I've got to say he seemed nice he made coffee and we listened to albums talking about his life in New York and, his family. After the first few weeks I noticed some control issues he had. We were sitting on the porch one day as a friend went by i waved and Jack said why did you wave to him who the hell is he. I proceeded to tell him that he was not my boyfriend and that was the first time I saw pure evil in his eyes. He said you're my damn girl and, I want you to marry me. I said, "No, we have only known each other 3 weeks." Well at that time he took the time to try and act like a real man; being nice, taking me places. His dad drove us around because neither of us had a driver's license at the time. I thought he liked me because he wanted to spend every minute with me. It was a very hot and steamy day and Jacks dad wanted to know if we wanted to go to the beach with him.

We went to the ocean, I had shorts on almost to my knees and, a short sleeve button down shirt. Nothing was revealed. Jack really had a hard time with this because his dad said to me, "You look good."

Jack and I were walking alone on the beach and he said, "I don't want to marry a whore so if that's what you want to dress like you can fuckin' walk home. We were 25 miles from home so I said. "Would you like to have me change my clothes?" He said, "Yes."

He had been drinking straight vodka all day and, as I proceeded to the changing rooms he said, "Hey, just because my father said you look good don't mean he wants to fuck you." I said, "I am not interested in your father so you shouldn't worry." I was told that if I ever told his father what he said he would deny it. It didn't matter because years later he did not hold back even in public. Humiliating me and degrading me especially in front of his family and, they would all join in.

We got back from the beach and I decided I wanted to go visit my mother and, tell her about Jack. I spoke to my friends and family about Jack wanting to marry me and him saying that loved me. I asked for their advice in the marriage.

They all thought he was a nice guy and said to do what I felt was best. What I did not know was that I would be allowed to see my mom only 3 more times within the next 20 years before she passed away.

What I really wanted to do was to never see him again but, I knew that would never happen. Within the next few weeks, I noticed him drinking a lot every day. I stayed away for a while. When I did, my friends and family would want to know why I was treating this guy so badly.

He had been talking to my siblings; crying about how much he loved me and couldn't live without me. I hadn't told anyone about his violence and how scared I was of him. I told them he was a heavy drinker and needed him to sober up or I wouldn't see him again.

About 2 months later, I was in my room cooking and watching TV. All of a sudden my door was kicked in. There was Jack drunk and very angry; he proceeded to enter my room. I told him get out and that I couldn't believe that he kicked my door open and broke my lock. I stopped babysitting full time because the lady moved away. I had not been at her house for a week. Jack started crying and sitting on my bed and said he missed me so much. He didn't even want to live without me. He asked me again to marry him. I said I would think about it just to get rid of him.

After he finally calmed down, I walked him home and went to school from there. When I lost my job the only way I could pay my rent was to get assistance from town office. The agreement was that I go back to school and they would pay my rent every month.

To my surprise, Jack was waiting for me every night and said he wanted to make sure I was safe getting home. While we were walking home he said, "I love you Shelby I don't want to live without you and I want to marry you." I said, "Listen, you really drink too much and I don't drink." Yes, I had drank in the past maybe 3-4 times but never with him. At that point he said he would quit and would never touch another drop if I married him.

He called his mom from a payphone because she lived in New York and told her we were getting married. She said, Don't get married yet I am coming to Maine 1 week later, Jack's dad went to pick her up at the airport and I waited at the apartment. When she walked into the apartment she looked at Jack and said, "No, this marriage will not ever happen. She is not good enough for and you can find someone prettier and better." Right in front of me, that really pissed me off. She stayed 2 days and left begging him not to marry me.

Chapter 2

Jack and Shelby's Wedding,
Broken Promises, Drug Use and
Physical violence

On February 27th, 1985 we got married.
Within hours of being married I was moved out
of my room and all my things were brought to
his apt. The town was also paying his rent
while he was supposed to be looking for a job
which never happened.

About 2 hours after our wedding a
friend of his came over and whispered
something in his ear. He looked at me and said
he would be right back. "Don't go anywhere or
let anyone in. Just make like you are not home
if anyone knocks." I thought that was odd.
When he returned from his friends he was
bragging about getting some LSD that day they
were going to hang out, drink, trip and have a
party. I said, "I thought you were going to quit
drinking if we got married." He slapped me so
hard that I went down. That was the first slap
and I knew from there I was in trouble.

The control was a lot in the first weeks
of marriage; Clothes he didn't like went into
the trash. So, I just thought he was a little
jealous and went along with it. I learned early
in the years with Jack to bite my tongue and not
stick up for myself.

After 1 month the drinking became
really intense and he refused to stay sober

enough to complete job search, which he never did.

CHAPTER 3 Jacks mom

Then out of the blue, Jacks mom says, "Come to New York for your honeymoon you can stay here." I told him why should I? She hates me and all she does is say how ugly I am and how her son could do better. Why would I?

We flew into LaGuardia airport and there was mama running to her baby boy with tears. Giving me dirty looks behind his back.

This 3 day trip was hell. The first night they both ganged up at me, telling me he should stay with her and I should be thrown out on the streets of queens and made to walk back to Maine they even drew me a road map to get to the highway. I was horrified. Are these people for real? Are they going to throw me out in these streets at night?

The answer was yes. Jack threw my coat at me and his mother held the door open. He then yelled don't let the door hit you on the ass on your way out.

I think this was one of my scariest moments in life. Tears just came pouring out I couldn't stop them. I turned around and

knocked on the door but, Jack's mother yelled, "If you don't get outta here I'm calling the cops." All I could hear was laughing after that.

When I stepped out into the hallway of the building I was thinking where do I go? I don't want to go walking in the streets of New York at midnight. So I decided to climb the 5 flights of stairs and hang out on the roof. What else could I do?

I sat on the edge of the building with my feet dangling looking at NYC all lit up and thought I hate this place. I was scared. I was thinking nobody would even care if I jumped and, would never have to hear them anymore. All I had to do was lean over and let go.

At that moment 4 teenagers came running onto the roof. One showed me his gun and I said that I needed to leave. I went back downstairs.

Lo and behold Jack came out to see where I was and told me to come in the house. I really hesitated; I didn't want to go in that house with those animals but, I was in a big city, 18 years old and, scared to death. He held my plane ticket.

For the next 3 hours they were drinking and laughing at me about wanting me to hitchhike back to Maine. Finally, it was bedtime and I did not want to lie near him and I was so sick I didn't want to be with him and my plan was that I was going to leave him. I'm done. I can't do this. I made a mistake. I got into bed, told him I was tired and wanted to sleep.

He wanted to watch Porno's. I don't watch Porno's. I don't like them and that's me. He was so plastered and all of a sudden he looks over and says you don't look that bad just put a paper bag over your head and you'd be fuckable. He told me: You know, you're my wife and a wife has to do whatever the husband wants in bed.

The fear that came over me was crazy. I actually started crying because he wanted to do sexual things that i was not comfortable with and I said no for 3 hours. Finally, I said, "Hey, I want to give you a surprise and pulled down his pants and gave him oral sex. I was so sick at that moment my stomach was turning but, I figured he has got to be ready to pass out soon. I take my time and within minutes, he had already made up his sick warped mind that he was getting what he wanted.

He grabbed me and threw me on the bed. I started crying saying please don't do this he said shut up or I will throw you out to the niggers, naked then watch and see what happens to you.

All I could think of was how could a human being do this to anyone? What's wrong with these people? I thought no meant no. I kept saying you're hurting me please stop. He would whisper in my ear: Shut the fuck up now or you will be out on your ass you fucking whore. You know you want it. Thank god he couldn't get it up. I just felt in fear thinking this sick bastard is enjoying himself and he was. I ran in the bathroom and took a long shower bawling sitting on the floor just wished I was dead for real.

The next 2 days I had to do what they said or I would be stuck in New York. On the last day we were headed to the airport. Mama called the airline to see if she could get her money back for the return flights. Of course, the answer was no. Thank god I was going home and I was going to run so far from him and his family.

Chapter 4

Back in Maine

The trip was very quiet we spoke maybe 2 times the whole flight I hated him. I felt so violated and so stupid and so ashamed. I wanted to disappear from everyone. When we arrived at the Portland jetport I was so happy that I was in Maine. I started crying with joy.

When he looked over at me he said, "What are you so happy for? Are you happy to be back home so you can leave me and go suck your boyfriends cock you whore?" "And don't even think about telling any of your family or friends about what happened in New York because if you shame me like that, I will slice your fucking throat from ear to ear." That was the first physical threat to my life and now I am petrified.

We got back to the apartment 3 days before the rent was due. Jack had already been working on a very long drunk. I was concerned thinking where are we going to live? I don't know why, I looked up and told him if we don't have an apt. I am going to move back in with my mom. He was tired from the flight and told me to make him something to eat. We sat down to eat and, he was so drunk. Out of nowhere he grabs my shirt and rips it off, ripped my bra off and had a very evil look on his face. He wasn't there, he was gone. I ran into the back room and looked for another shirt to put on when he came up behind me so fast I was very scared and shocked.

He grabbed me by the throat and threw me up against the bedroom wall. He said, "You fucking whore I will kill you if you ever leave me I swear it." He then unbuckled my pants with his hand still wrapped around my throat took my pants down.

He dragged me outside and threw me on the Porch naked and crying. I was so scared and wondered; what the hell did I do? Rehashing the day to see where I messed up because it had to be my fault.

After 3 hours naked on the Porch curled up in a ball and, only 20 degrees out he finally opened the door and said, "What did you do? Stand up and show everyone your twat you fucking slut I knew I married a whore."

About an hour later Jack passed out. Thank god. I went into the apartment and cleaned up , did the dishes.There was a knock at the door I was so scared to open it. His dad came over and I let him in. I told his father what he did to me and, he said, "You got to try to work it out. You are his wife." I looked at him and started to cry and said, "Why Rick? Why wouldn't you tell me how violent and psychotic he is?" He stood up and said, "You got him out my hair. He's a nasty bastard. Now I can live in peace for a while." He then stood up and said he was sorry and left.

I took a shower and went to bed. It took me hours to fall asleep as I was thinking of how to get the hell out of this torture house. Finally I decided I dont want to be here anymore .The landlord stopped by the next day and gave me an eviction notice saying we had 30 days to move .We packed up. Jacks dad had a camp on Cobbossee Lake and he said all the tourists have gone home so it is very private with no neighbors. He told me the store is 4.1 miles away but that he would be there every week to take us shopping. I thought oh no I am now moving into this camp how am I going to get away? I am screwed. I will have to wait till his dad takes us in town, wait until I am within a

1/2 mile from a Police department and make a run for it.

About 6 days later Jacks dad showed up this was the big day. I wanted to leave and I was doing it we got into Augusta and stopped at a video game store and I got out of the car and I ran across the bridge to the Police station.

When I get to the Police station and I told them everything about New York. I said he is hurting me and I wanted him arrested. They said, "Calm down and take a seat someone will be with you shortly." So I sat down and got the most eerie feeling up my spine.

As I stood up and turned my head there was Jack, standing in the front doorway of the Police station. He was mad. I have never seen such an evil face in my life. I am struck with bone chilling fear, I'm frozen, my legs can't move and, am speechless but, the tears won't stop. I turned around and said, "If I walk out that door with him I am dead."

The detective came in and said, "What's the problem? The officer told the detective were having a lovers spat" then they both chuckled. At that moment I could feel Jack standing behind me. He turned me around, leaned over and said, "I was to turn around and tell them I made a mistake, put your arm around me and walk out or I'll snap your fucking neck right here." I was paralyzed and so scared for my life.

I was supposed to be safe in a Police station. I'm not safe. I am stuck. He will forever hunt me down and kill me so; I turned around and said, "This is a mistake." Then the cop looked at the detective and said, "See they are all made up." "Have a good night." Jack threw his arm around me and said, "Let's go home babe we need to talk." We went back to camp and he acted like nothing ever happened. He kept thinking about me getting away and it drove him crazy and the violence started coming out worse by the day .

He would get very angry and throw coffee tables and, smash coffee cups. Throw plates of food and say my cooking sucked. Then he'd say, "Go clean that up you fucking ugly pig and get the fuck out of my face." I really wanted to tell him I wanted out but, he wouldn't listen, and just to throw a note out there. Jack's mom and dad supported his drinking habit for years. That's why he never ran out. They were afraid to say no.

We were only married for 6 weeks when we moved to the camp. Jacks drinking did not stop in fact, it got worse. Dad was making sure he would always leave 2 gallons of vodka and, he traded food stamps for them. So there was never a shortage of liquor.

April 1986 was a very bitterly cold month. Temps were 25 below zero days and colder at nights. I was begging him to either find a job or let me get my GED so I could work and get out of this camp I did not like it.

He looked at me and said you are not going to work so you can find someone else to fuck.

At that point I knew there was going to be a fight so I said forget it.

He was gone again; just a look of pure evil and grinding his teeth. I knew he was coming after me. I ran into the living room and he grabbed me by the hair of my head and threw me on the floor ripped off my shirt and tore my pants right off me. He told me, "Get the fuck up cunt. You ran to the cops on me you ugly fucking mutt." "What did you tell them?" Reminding me about the Police station and keep in mind he would use this for the start of so many fights year after year. I said, "I told them nothing." He said, "You fucking lying whore."

I stood up naked in the unheated living room it was probably 20 degrees in that room he told me to open the front door and threw me towards the screen. I flew face first naked in 2 feet of snow. I turned around crying and he said, "When you are ready to tell the truth about what you told the cops then I will let you in."

There was no place to go. These were seasonal camps only. I couldn't walk anywhere I was naked and I was so cold. In what seemed like hours but, was about 25 minutes he opened the door and said, "Get me something to eat. I'm tired and hungry." He stated that if I tried to run again he and his father had made plans to kill me and bury me in the woods. I believed him so I got him something to eat and he passed out immediately after.

I realized that I had come to a point in my life where I was stuck with him. He wasn't letting me get away. I believed every threat he made to me and would do if I tried to leave him again. So, I had to try to make the best out of it until I found a way out.

We stayed in that camp until June because, by then the tourist were there and Jacks dad was getting complaints about fighting and screaming all hours of the night.

Chapter 5

An Apartment in town

Jack's father was going to pay for rent and deposit to get us out of his camp. So, he found us a 2 bedroom apt. in Fairfax. I was 2 months pregnant at that time and, having a very hard pregnancy. He was screaming and yelling every day for nothing. If I said hi to the neighbor I was a slut and got hit.

Even the pregnancy didn't stop him. Mostly he'd smack me in the head and spit in my face as he said, "I always got what I deserved." He was drunk every day.My doctor

told me that because Jack drank so much there is risk of fetal development delay. I thought I was prepared to have a child. NO I was not. Now granted, I love children. Having a child with him I knew there would be issues and there were.

Chapter 6

The Baby

When Jack jr. was born he was breech so I had to have a cesarean section. Which, by the way, he and his mother laughed about. Later calling me a wimp and for not handling the pain and not being a real woman doing natural childbirth.

As you know my mother in law had to come see her son's boy. My first night from the hospital all night long they were talking about that they should take the baby back to New

York and raise him there. I stood up from the couch and looked her and said, "I am calling the cops and I am going to tell them you two are going to kidnap my baby and bring him to New York."

His mom handed the baby to Jack and started walking towards me, keep in mind I just got out of the hospital and had a 10 inch cut

from a c section and had tons of stitches as she came seemingly out of nowhere and shoved me with all her might into the corner. I hit the wall hard and I thought wow she had some strength. She looked down at me and pointed her finger in my face saying, "I've got enough money that I can buy a lawyer and get full custody of the baby and have your ass sent to the insane hospital for the rest of your life but, first I will tell the Police you are suffering from postpartum and we want you evaluated for suicide and we believe that I might try to kill the baby." They also were going to accuse me of incest. I just looked into those dark evil eyes and could not believe that she said that.

I stood up and went outside to smoke a cigarette. Now I'm really screwed I thought. I am going to die with this animal. I wasn't getting out alive. I went in the house made a coffee and watched TV while Jack and his mother were getting drunk the last night before she was headed back to New York.

Having a child with him was awful. He became insanely jealous and twisted. I could not breastfeed my son because Jack said that it was sick and I was sick in the head. The word he used was incest. So, he called all 3 of his family members while of course he is drunk as hell and tells them I was sick because I was getting turned on by it.

I was so sick to my stomach and speechless. Formula it was. After months had passed I felt so trapped and scared. Every time I would get up out of bed he would jump up still drunk and accuse me of leaving him for another man. He actually convinced himself that I was going to take the baby and run. That didn't sound like a bad idea to me. We didn't last too long at the apt.

I didn't have enough money from my check to pay the bills because his booze came first. So I signed up for town assistance and they helped for 3 months and then said they couldn't help us anymore unless Jack worked community service work to pay it off 40 hours a week for rent and utilities. Of course that was a no go.

I had to lie and tell the town that Jack and I separated so they would agree to help me with the bills. 3 months later the Police had been over to our house so many times that we got evicted and they were called about fighting yelling crying furniture being thrown and extremely loud music.

Chapter 7

Back to Camp… Again

So we ended up back at the camp for the winter no water, no toilet, no electricity and no heat except for a small kerosene stove and now with a baby. Going to the bathroom in a trash bag was horrible and it was so cold there, now granted the kerosene heater kept the one

room warm but, that's where we spent the winter.

I had enough of the camp living and I wanted a hot shower and heat. So, when as usual Jack and his dad had taken off and wanted to try the new seafood place in Auburn they said I wasn't welcome. He didn't have the money to pay for me so I stayed home ..

Usually when they went out to eat once a month I waited in the car with the baby till they were done. I weighed 98 pounds at the time; while I had time I decided to call a church in Wayne and told them my story.

They put me on a waiting list for free housing. It was another year stuck at the camp.

Jacks drinking had been binges that would last months. Up to this point it had been 2 years since we got married and he showed no interest in working. Finally I got a call from the church. They had a three bedroom mobile home on their own property. The only thing I had to do was put my name into a rent subsidy program and I could stay there for free. No drugs or alcohol or we would be evicted.

I thought to myself if I could keep him away from the booze that diluted his mind maybe we could try to go on with life. Even sober I have never seen anyone so controlling and so nasty. I couldn't go to bed unless he went. If I started to make something to eat I was a fat fuck and he didn't want no fat bitch. It was bad enough he had an ugly one so, you can only try to imagine.

I had lost all my self esteem. No naps if I got tired whenever I said anything to defend myself he would threaten to call his dad to bring him booze. I would back off and, let him run off at the mouth. He was such a spoiled, mean, ruthless and entitled person that most of the time I would just walk away.

I liked taking baths especially after living in that camp. One night I fell asleep in the tub when the door was kicked open. He said, "What the fuck are you doing?" "I am fucking hungry get your fat ugly ass out the tub and make me something to eat." I grabbed a towel and shut the door. I guess I had been in the bath for 25 minutes or so. I got dressed and I made him something to eat and what scared me the most was he hadn't drank for a year plus. That tells me it's not the booze at all. This is him the real deal. I am living with a monster.

Chapter 8

Depression

At this time in my life I use to cry every night and pray for the hell to stop. Sometimes I would just dream that I would wake up and he was dead and my life could go on. What did I do to deserve this life? Was I that bad of a person? I became utterly depressed. I started suffering from massive migraines that lasted 6-7 Days and he didn't care the music went louder. He would always say, "I can do whatever the fuck I want and you can't stop me.

I even started thinking about taking my life. Then I would think: I can't leave that baby with this animal. The first chance I get to leave him I am outta here.

The stress and putdowns were horrendous. I was physically, emotionally wrecked. There was so much that happened to me. He was so abusive and I feared for my life every day. I hated having sex with him but if I didn't I went through hell. It was awful.

The trailer didn't last too long. Someone with 3 kids needed shelter so we went back to that camp again. Well it came time to get out of the camp. The Police had showed up 3 times in a week and the neighbors were complaining and he was threatening to kill all of them. So, Rick again got us an apt in Auburn and just dropped us off. Well that didn't go so well because Jack did not stop drinking and the liquor store was right around the corner. We lived in this apt. until the cops started coming again.

The landlord came over and knocked on the door. He said, "I need to evict you. Too many complaints from neighbors and the Police have been here every other day." People didn't like him so he stood in the doorway. Jack comes out of the bedroom, drunk as hell and said, "Who the fuck do you think you are?" The landlord showed Jack his gun that he had strapped. Jack looked at him and said, "Are you threatening me? Jack just smiled ear to ear. The most evil grin I have ever seen. I took the eviction notice and shut the door.

I just knew something was up. Jack turned to me and said, "I want you go to the Police department and tell them he tried to rape you by gunpoint." My jaw dropped. I was speechless. I could never do this omg why would he say that?

It turned out that throughout the next 17 years he used this method threaten his mom and dad into giving him booze money. Telling his father that I would say that he tried to rape me. I told him I wouldn't do it and he slapped me across the face open handed so that it left a mark. I wasn't allowed to leave the house till the marks went away. He chuckled to himself and said, Next time I'll smack you upside the head in case you get any bright ideas about calling the cops." I didn't want to add 13 years to this 20 year hell.

Jack was on probation for loud music , threatening the Police, domestic violence, assault and he had been arrested numerous times but, mommy and daddy wouldn't allow their baby to stay in jail so they would bail him out every time. He had violated his probation at least 50 times and he always got just a slap on the wrist.

After a few years of being with this animal; Jacks two sisters started telling me how violent he had always been toward his mom and dad. When he was 14 he told his mom to go get booze because mama always had liquor in the house. He always drank it and when mom said no he would beat the shit out of her. He would keep kicking her in the stomach until she would give in.

When Jacks mom called one day he was out back drinking and I asked her about the incident. She said it was all lies the girls were very jealous of Jack being the only boy and the baby of the family. I knew all along they were telling the truth.

I also learned that Jacks mom and sisters would talk to me and then report this to Jack I had nobody. His family hated me.

That next day the Maine Housing Authority called and they found a 2 bedroom apt. right down the road and I only had to pay 65 dollars a month heat and lights included. I contacted Jacks dad and said we need help moving. He came down and we moved into a duplex in Auburn. With the extra money from the check, Jack took it for himself.

He wouldn't give me anything for personal items. He never bought anything for me or the baby. Clothes were sent by his mom for him and the baby so they were all set. Me as long as the baby had what he needed I was okay.

Chapter 9

New Neighbors

The fighting ceased for a little while in the new place. New tenants that were partiers moved in I want to say 7 months later. A couple with a 3 year old child moved in. The man and his wife immediately were invited on the back Porch for a party they were drunks so there they were.

I went out back and set up the play pen outside for the baby it was a nice day while I was out there the playpen got stuck so I asked Jack to give me a hand with it. Instead the new guy jumped off the Porch and said, "I will help you sweetheart." I cringed and immediately looked at Jacks face. I saw the evil grin and knew there was going to be the first blowout in the new place.

I knew the only place we had left to move is in that camp he wasn't going to work ever. So any ways as the 2 new neighbors are getting drunk he keeps just staring at me. I was so scared.

When the party started dying down we went inside, Jack said, "I saw how you were staring at his cock every fucking minute you couldn't keep your eyes off it." "What a fucking whore you are to do that shit in front of your husband." "Shame me like that."

That's when he punched me in the head so hard I fell to the floor and hit hard. He said, "Now go to the cops and show them the fuckin' bruises. There ain't none." Jack just laughed. That was the first fist hit.

He proceeded to tell me as I was lying on the floor crying that the neighbors were swingers and the man wanted to know if we would join them in an orgy, I just gasped in disgust and said, "No way." He said," I think we should do it. Why don't you go up there and suck his cock you fuckin' whore." "You know that's what you want to do."

I got up someone called the cops and I think it was the upstairs couple. They could hear every word.

The next day Jacks dad came over and Jack told his dad, "We need to move back down to the camp because his wife was a whore." And, he couldn't have any friends because my wife will fuck them all because she's a fucking pig. Dad said, "No sorry, I will help you move but not back to my camp it's too shameful having you around."

Chapter 10

Auburn to Augusta

I contacted the Maine Housing Authority and needed to be put on the list for housing in the Augusta area. They told me I was very lucky. A third floor, 2 bedroom with heat and lights included apartment was available and I would only have to pay 125.00 a month. I told them I would take it. Well, on the move again probation had to be transferred to Augusta.

I liked it lots of people in the building I thought I might be safe for a while. We moved and things were a little better. I met a sweet lady across the street one day she was taking all her groceries in and I ran over and helped her into the house she said, "I see you walking a lot; you have no car." I said, "I have no license." She said, "We are going to change that, every Monday and Wednesday I want you to come over at 9am and we are going to practice driving."

Jack thought it was great but, also said, "You're so fucking stupid you will never get it." I was bound and determined to prove him and his family wrong. Well, he was right I failed, parallel parking got me. But, the teacher said to sign up for a new date and I'd get it. So, I did. I went home and, of course became the laughing stock of the family. I felt stupid.

In next 4 weeks to follow, the neighbor told me to practice with her for 3 days a week she was convinced I could do it. The day came wow was I nervous but, I was doing it this time and I did it as soon as the driving test was over and he said congratulations your licensed. I started crying happy and what was the best was I could go home and say fuck you all I did it. Pardon the language I didn't like to swear but I was happy.

Jack called his mom and said I probably went on a side road and sucked his cock in order to get it. Well, I didn't. I swear nothing could bring me down I was so happy.

The next thing was getting a car. Jacks dad was tired of helping out so he decided to help me find my first car and we did. What a lemon that was. We went to the DMV to get it legal his dad paid $400 for it. On the way to the garage to have it looked at after dad bought it, I was pulled over and the officer wanted to impound saying it was illegal for the road and, thank god right across the street was the garage. He agreed to let me move it across the street and told the garage owner he wanted the car looked over and safe before it left the shop.

When they got it on the lift, the car was a rust bucket. The muffler fell right off as he touched it. He said the car is no good and couldn't be driven. I called Jack and he said, "The guys at the garage were fucking crooks." I said he's not charging me. Jack told me bring the car and get back home now we will call somebody else. The owner of the garage said, "I can't let you drive this car; it's not safe someone's going to get killed. I said, "Yes that would be me if I don't get this car and me home now." He handed me the keys and told me to take the back street home I was only 1/2 mile from my apt so it was a quick ride.

When I walked in Jack started screaming at me. I said, "Your dad bought the car not me." I got the info about the car from the previous owner and called him. I told him he needed to pick up this car and, I want my money back. "He said I'll talk with my wife and call you back." I got no response for 4 days. Finally I called him back and said, "The Police want to know the name of the previous owner so they can be charged with an illegal sticker." I told him at that point I would call the cops with the info. 24 hours later he returned with the money and, picked up the car.

We were back to find another vehicle. It was back to dad helping until we found something else.

Chapter 11

Antiques and Jacks Psychosis

One day, Jacks dad came over on a Saturday at 7 am. I was just getting up . He asked us if we wanted to go to some lawn sales. He would loan us 10 dollars. I was thrilled. We got into the car. I enjoyed lawn sales and, I loved old stuff. The lawn sales were great.

We stopped at several. I spent 4 dollars on some costume jewelry and a piece of ugly pottery. I had to fight to get it but, I told Jack they threw it in the pile so I paid nothing. Truth Was, I paid 1.00 for it because it looked real old. Well living in the antique capital of the state I figured I would take the stuff I got and go see what it was worth.

The day went by and I was thinking of ways to make extra money. I told Jack what my plans were and he agreed which was shocking well the first shop I stopped at I met a man by the name of Arnold. He and his boyfriend had just opened up an antique shop. I went in and fell in love with the stuff right there. I wanted in this business so, I asked him does he buy stuff and he said, "whatcha got honey?" I always loved the way he said it he was so sweet. It was actually shocking to meet someone that was not like Jacks family. They were all I ever hung around with for family.

My family members were not allowed in the house. He told me that he would smash any member of family in the face if they ever came to see me. So I just didn't tell them where I lived throughout the years and lost touch. I didn't need the headaches.

I paid 4.00 for the stuff and Arnold asked me what I wanted for all of it. I said, "Make me a good offer." He said, "I will give you $100.00." Wow, I was so excited. I wanted to go to lawn sales again. I ran home and showed Jack the $50 I made. On the way home I deposited $50 in my bank account so I would have money to go to lawn sales the next weekend with my own money. I later told him I had the account and said. "Every week I want to go find stuff and sell it to the shops." Jack couldn't believe it.

I told him Arnold wanted to come up to the house to have coffee and drop off some books about antiques and collectibles. I warned Jack that he was gay.

Now a lot of stuff isn't written about as far as prejudice and racism are concerned. I want to tell you this is the most racist family I had ever met and I refuse to use that language or those words. They hated anyone different, not just gays.

Jack started telling me stories about gay bashing that I had no clue existed. He told me one story about how he lured a male hooker in an alley and, stabbed the hooker with a pen knife he said that had a 2 inch blade. Jack said, "Give up your money and jewelry and I'll will let you live." The man started to scream. Jack ran but, this guy followed him. Jack was getting close to his home and hid around the corner. Then he said he turned and stabbed him several times and said, "I told you to stop following me." Jack said. "I think he died but, nobody cared because of what he was."

There was a stray kitten hanging around and I could tell she was starving. I was feeding it. On about the 3rd day I decided to take her upstairs and told jack I would bring it to the animal shelter. He said, "No keep it." So I did but, I shouldn't have. Jack hated animals. He had a BB gun and, one night he shot her in the face. The BB got lodged under her eye. I was crying. Jack said, "It's only a fucking cat, what the fuck are you crying for." I brought the cat to the shelter and said that I found her. I walked away thinking no more animals in the house ever.

I was really scared about inviting Arnold over but, I wanted to show Jack that the man was gay and I was just selling antiques to him. Arnold came over and it was fun; him telling us about what to look for.

I was really into it, I found my passion. I was good not to pat myself on the back but damn I was good, every week going out to lawn sales selling and adding to the bank account. Soon and I don't remember how long maybe 6 months I had $1000 in my account. Jack knew about every penny because he held the check book and the money. I sat down one morning and told Jack I want to buy a house. I had no credit but his mom had told him she would cosign the house if we had the down payment and made payments each month

Well, the next weekend; Jacks dad came over to take us out to lawn sales. I brought my sons booster seat down and set him in the car seat and buckled him up. I could smell the booze on him and I didn't want to go. I started arguing with his dad that claimed he was sober.

I buckled my son in and all of a sudden the car started and I went under the wheel right in front of my house. I was lying on the ground crying. I knew my foot was broke.

Jack told me, "Shut the fuck up and get upstairs and that I fucked the whole day up." I couldn't stand up and I fell right down. Jack looks at his dad and said, "I've got to carry this fat fucking bitch up 3 flights of stairs thanks a lot dad."

Jacks dad left and I needed to get to the hospital after I was carried up. He says, "If you go to the hospital don't tell them anything about my father I will take care of my father don't worry. I had to take a cab go to the hospital. I had 3 broken bones and a cast and crutches. I told them the truth so I could have it on record.

The next couple of days went by and Jack was getting restless. He had to stay sober because his probation officer was starting to piss test him. Jack got up one morning and said, "Watch and see what I do he called his dad and

told him to give him 5000 dollars or he was
going to the Police and tell them you were
drunk when you ran her over." "She's sticking
with my story." He told his son to fuck off and
he didn't come around for a long time. I filed
an insurance claim and sued his ass.

When the insurance company called he
said the maximum I could get from the case
was 10 thousand because that was all he was
insured for. I took it. There's the down
payment for the house, welfare payments,
covered the mortgage and all the bills. Because
Jack was never going to work.

The first thing we had to do was buy a
car because now we were taking cabs. So, it
was decided we had to pay at least $2500 for a
vehicle and buy it from a dealership. I took a
cab to the car mall and there it was. Fresh on
the lot, a 1989 tan Ford Tempo mint interior
80k miles was a lot but I wanted it. It had brand
new sticker and was ready to go.

I asked how much is that car going to be
when it got on the lot he said let me find out
throws me the keys and tells me to take it for a
ride and see how I like it. I loved it; perfect size
easy to drive and clean. The salesman came
back out 10 minutes later and said we have to
get $4900 for it. I said no too much it's got
high mileage (like I knew anything about cars
but, it was working.) I stood up looked at the
salesman and said, "this is how it is, I have
2500 dollars cash in my pocket I want that car
like nothing else and I want everything." "Tax,
title and doc fees thrown in the 2500 and if
can't do this in the next 10 minutes I will go
elsewhere."

The salesman came out and tried to get
more money telling me they would lose money

at that cost I started to get up and he said,
"You've got 2500 in cash right now?" I said,
"Yes." I pulled a wad of all hundreds out and
he said let me go wave this money under his
nose let me try one more time I said, "I'm
leaving with or without the car."I think I grew
something that day I was pretty proud of
myself even more so when the owner came out
and said, "You've got a set of balls lady. I've
got to hand it to you if you ever want a job call
me." He shook my hand and said, "The car is
yours you earned it."

I was so happy. My very first car and, in
own my name alone. It felt so good. I started
going to lawn sales every weekend and decided
to broaden my horizons and find some more
dealers to sell to. I went to other antique shops
see what they wanted to pay, because I was
new. I learned quickly and I started talking to
dealers I invited some up. This was helping my
new found business.

Jack had stopped drinking so he needed
something to do. Finally one Day I told Jack I
wanted to post an ad in the paper looking to
buy coins and jewelry and antiques to see what
would happen. He agreed. It worked. I got lots
of calls, most were junk but got some good
gold items rings ect.

The money was coming in we still had
the 10 grand for the down payment and I
started tucking a few dollars here and there to
help get us through Christmas and snow tires
that I didn't tell him about. Trust me I didn't
get rich.

Chapter 12

Control Freak

I found school clothes for my son that were not planned for. Well, Jack refused to dip into the money again. We had already payed off for the tempo within 5 or 6 weeks. Business was booming and I thought maybe he will be a good person now but in reality name calling and control about eating and sleeping was a daily habit for him. If I was 10 minutes late Jack would scream and fight.

He'd call his mom, he would scream, "Mom I got a fuckin' whore for a wife I am sick of this shit." And other things like that. I still felt his noose around my neck and was struck with fear living with him. I know I had a car and license and that I should've left.

Why didn't I leave? Well first of all I was never allowed anywhere with the boy he had to be with the baby, at all times even at the Wic and welfare office. He would wait in the car. He always demanded my car keys from me every night. He knew it was only a matter of time before i would try to run again. So I just focused on antiques. I ran ads to buy coins and jewelry.

Within a week of the ad running on the last day I got a call from a man that was a collector of coins and old bottles.

We were interested so I explained the directions to get to my apt and 30 minutes later there was a knock at the door. His name was Jeremy he had a cigar box full of coins and a box of old bottles. He was 6 feet tall looked like he hadn't bathed ever; stunk and was filthy from head to toe. Jack ran up to him invited him in and shook his hand.

Jack told me, "Don't just fucking stand there looking stupid make some fucking coffee."Then it dawned on me right there he is losing it because he wouldn't treat me like that in front of anyone before. That's why nobody believed me. So I knew he was boiling up inside from no booze and I knew soon he would snap again. I just didn't know when.

I stayed in the other room after I made coffee and I could hear whispering low. I couldn't make out what was being said at all. About an hour later, Jack came out and said, "Give Jeremy a ride home so he won't have to pay $5 for a cab." I said I need to talk to you and we went into the bathroom and I said, "You bring him home." I said, "I don't trust him. "What if he attacks me? "We don't know him." He said, "You are going. I am not getting dressed it will be fine. He's coming back with some cool antiques in 2 days he's got to dig them out." So I drove him home and asked him how started getting into collecting. He was talking so fast that I couldn't understand him. He was sniffling constantly. I thought he had a sinus problem. I asked him if he needed a tissue. There some in the glove box if you do. He said, "No I'm fine."

I dropped him off without incident and, headed back home. When I walked in Jack said, "What did you two talk about?" I said, "He was talking about how he became a collector. Jack proceeded to say that this man is in love with Hitler. He's fucking awesome. I felt like I wanted to puke right there.

I knew Jack and his family were racists but when Jack was telling stories about concentration camps; this guy was getting excited. I said, "Never speak to him again and,

I don't want him in my house with my son.
This man is not right, up there. He's a
psychopath." 2 Days later the call that I
dreaded came. I heard an overly excited Jack
say, "Ok buddy see ya in a few.

I put my head down and knew I was
going to have to go get him and, bring him
back to my place so I could listen to 2 morons
talk about death camps; Naming off generals of
the SS and the Luftwaffe. They talked for hours
and I noticed sniffing noises and every time
Jack came into the living room he was all fired
up talking 200 words a minute. I knew there
were drugs involved. They hung out for 6 hours
snorting pills and Jeremy said, "He had to get
home." They whispered to each other about
something.

I found out later Jeremy was given 120
Ritalin a month and Jack was going to buy half
of them every month so Jeremy could have
extra cash. He lived on disability and was being
treated at the veteran's hospital for
physiological problems caused from the war.
They were filling him full of pills. He didn't
snort every day. He had other pills he took.

Chapter 12

Jack Gets Arrested… Almost

Jack got addicted to Ritalin staying up
48-72 at a time; no eating and wouldn't let
anyone sleep. I was so exhausted and he was
losing the rest of his mind he would tell me,
"You have been gone for 6 hours, where the
fuck have you been?" I said, "I have been gone

20 minutes. I just went to the bank like you said." Then, fighting and screaming for 4 hours till finally he realized I was right.

He was coming down off the pills and decided to go to bed. The next day was his visit to his probation officer and Jack was getting piss tested for alcohol so he was real nervous. I said, "Don't they have to give different kinds of tests for drugs like a blood test?" Hell, I didn't know but I was hoping this test covered everything and it did.

While Jack and I were sitting in the office waiting for the drug test results. The door opened his Probation officer came out and said Jack stand up put your hands behind your head you are under arrest you tested positive for drugs and he put the handcuffs on and told me to come with him.

"The PO sat behind his desk and said, "Are you doing drugs ? I could throw your ass in jail but I'm not going to because you have a wife and child but you will see me 2 times a month and you will be tested every time you see me until your probation is over. Do you understand?" Jack said, "Sir I am so sorry it won't happen again." I slipped. He stood up, walked around and took the cuffs off Jack and said, "You're free to go." I was appalled I said, "What a justice system." I never had any faith in Police after the Police station incident anyway. So, we got in the car and headed home.

Jack was laughing, saying how he fucked over the law and how good he was at getting away with shit. I personally called him a suck pump. So now he had to pace himself he found out from Jeremy you could buy a product and it would clean you out of every drug and

alcohol in hours but you got to start drinking
gallons of water 2 days in advance so they
figured out what days they could snort and
when he had to start cleaning up.

He was snorting speed 22 days a
month and it worked out good because the
doctors started writing the script in half every
two weeks because he didn't make it the month
so there was plenty for Jack and they met like
clockwork.

Chapter 13

Jacks Karma

Well, by that time we had got quite a
few coins in a collection and a large album with
some key dates. Up until now we had decided
he was never to see the album. I still didn't
trust him but, apparently Jeremy tricked Jack
and said, "I've got some rare coins in my
pocket." Jack said, "Well if you show me yours
I will show you my collection." I just thought,
how stupid. So Jack yells to me, "Hey go get
the album now and bring it to me. I'm doing
business here; move it." "What the fucks wrong
with you?" Jeremy thought that was funny, so
as you can see they were friends till the end.

Well Jack went to the bathroom and I
was on the couch I could see him flipping the

pages what I didn't see is that he stole my
1938d walking liberty half dollar. He closed the
book and stood up and said, "I guess I forgot
my coins on the counter." I will bring them
next week."

I had to give him a ride home .When I
walked back through the door home Jack was
pacing all around the house. He was very mad,
he said, "The prick stole the 38d walker." I
said, "I told you there was something wrong
about him." I asked him, do you want to go to
the Police?" He said, "Fuck no, I'd get no more
pills then I'd have go to the store and buy a half
gallon of vodka."

I don't know too much about booze
but, I did know that when he drank vodka; he
was gone from earth, entirely blacked out. I
really believed he didn't know. At least that's
what I wanted to believe. So he said, "I will get
him back and I am never going to mention the
coin." I said, "Why? He stole it he's a thief."

He said, "He could go to the cops and
say Jack stole his pills and get him arrested. So
the hair brained idea to get him back was the
next time he comes over we run a coffee pot of
water through the machine and put 15 dieters
tea bags in it 1 hour before I went to get him.

Jack insisted that Jeremy have a cup of
tea and Jacks mom sent him 10 boxes of a
dieter's tea you drink once a day so he figured
Jeremy loved coffee and tea and always drained
the pot. So, when I arrived Jack took the largest
coffee mug and poured a very dark tea added
sugar and cream and said, "I made a special pot
just for you buddy."

I thought wow, that's payback. I knew
he wasn't going to mess up the pill deal he had
no other place to get them. Jack kept pumping

the tea to him. Finishing the 10 cup pot about
30 minutes later.

Jeremy stood up and said, "I've got to
go. I've got a stomach ache and feel sick."
Jack said see you in 2 weeks. Of course what
he really cared about was getting the pills.
Well, I took him home the 15 minute ride and
as he was getting out of the car he soiled
himself and started swearing. I told him well it
must have been something you ate.

I went home and told Jack what
happened and he started laughing and said,
"That will teach him." I didn't see how.

Well that weekend I decided to check
out a few lawn sales and maybe stop in a few
shops to see what was selling. I ended up at
Arnolds shop he stated that he just got his real
estate license and I told him I was looking for a
2 or 3 bedroom home in Kennebec county gave
him the specifics I was looking for and he went
to work.

Chapter 14

Buying a House

Well about 1 month later I got a call. A
piece of property was going on the market and
the owner was dying so she wanted to sell the
house to give the money to her son before she
goes.

I told Jack and he refused to even leave
the house at this point he became obsessed with
Ritalin. So I went to see the property myself. I
loved it, it was perfect. 1/2 a duplex and it had

3 bedrooms and large back yard front yard
just outside of town a few neighbors not far
from the Police department and right next door
is a phone booth just in case.

So while Jack refused to go, I set up
everything I went to the closing alone nobody
ever saw the house till we moved in. His mom
cosigned and I had the $10000 to lay down and
I was still getting welfare. The payments were
low for the house with insurance included it
was $197 a month. After the closing I told Jack
we need more money I want to replace doors
and some windows and do some cosmetic
work.Time for me to get a job.

I applied at a clothing store and, a
supermarket . The clothes store called first and
said you're hired. 6.75 An hour. I was reluctant
but thrilled to work and get out of the house. As
I was walking out of the house the phone rang.

The shopping mall called and they
wanted me for $1an hour more. I told them I
was sorry. I got hired elsewhere. I began
working 30 hours a week to start, then 40 as I
got better. For some reason I enjoyed working
with the public so I was good at my job. I still
went to lawn sales on the weekend.

I started to do a flea market. I was able
to make $200 or $300 a week just selling stuff.
Jewelry was my thing and I enjoyed it. I had a
busy outside life and it didn't take long for
Jack to show his true colors there about 2
months of peace but he was always so nasty
whenever I got home telling me I must be
having affairs out there behind his back.
Another quick note I am very old fashioned just
like my mom and I do not believe in cheating
no matter how bad the situation is. I have had

men confront me and I told them straight out I am married.

Ever since I was 13 years old all I wanted was to marry a man who treated me good and spend the rest of my life with him. Unfortunately that didn't happen and it never would. Jack had 6 months left on his probation which meant he could do whatever he wanted drugs, alcohol, whatever.

I was scared because if he started drinking I was done work for sure. Within this 6 months. Jack decided he was going to call all his drinking buddies and people he got pills from and invite them over. I was in trouble. My 1996 car had died. I went back to same place and got another one. A 1992 grand marquis. All the way up to the last day of probation I was warned several times by Jack that on the way home from his last PO meeting he was getting a bottle of vodka.

Chapter 15

Jack starts drinking again

Here we go. He had kept a lot of stuff bottled up inside because I used to threaten him if he touches me again I am going to the cops. I had enough I had bruises all over my body. I was hurting.

So, the day came and just as he promised he got a 1/2 gallon of vodka.

It was my day off thank god but it didn't matter I was getting it tonight and I knew it. Within hours he had 3 people there with all kinds of pills. Zanax and pain meds. They were

sitting around snorting pills and drinking
straight vodka when he started to get hammered
which didn't take long

He was yelling constantly in front of his
friends, "Get in here and get my friends a beer
and now you fucking bitch where are your
manners?"

Apologizing to his friends and saying,
"How ashamed he was of me." Laughing and
telling his friends that he didn't know why he
married me. I was a lazy bitch and he could
only fuck me with a paper bag over my head.
Hell, that didn't bother me anymore it was said
too many times.

I did as I was told and toward the end of
the night I needed to go to bed because I had to
go to work in the morning. We now had 5
people in the house and it was midnight and the
stereo was cranking. Nobody could sleep. I
went downstairs and told Jack I have to get up
for work in 6 hours could he please turn the
music down. Here comes the evil finally even
in front of his friends. He stood up and said,
"I'll do whatever the fuck I want. You don't
like it bitch get the fuck out of my house, this is
my house my mother cosigned for it and left it
to me. You can get the fuck out but you're not
taking my son." First of all he hated everyone
including his son.

I went upstairs he came up and ripped
all the blankets off me, smashed at 4:30 am
yelling at me to make him something to eat. I
did.

I may have gotten 1 hour of sleep so I
called my boss and lied and said I got diarrhea
and can't come in but I don't want to lose my
hours and he said, "Ok. I Made Jack something
to eat but, by the time I got upstairs he had

passed out.Good, I had a couple of hours to get some rest which was rare. I ended up cleaning the mess from his friends.

When Jack woke up he was sick as a dog and he would just throw up all over the house. Never even trying to make it to the bathroom how disgusting. He said, "I feel like shit." The guys were gone. No more pills so, we fought for hours. He wanted more booze I told him, "I can't work and have you drunk all day with my son."

He said, "Fuck you. You don't take care of him. I raised him myself you dumb fucking whore." "My mother and sisters will testify against you saying you are unfit so if you don't get me that bottle I will get it myself and then watch and see what happens." Then you are going to pay. Fear, the most horrible feeling to have every day of your life but, that's how I lived every day for 20 years. I knew I had no choice he would have got it himself and it would be worse.

He got drunk quick and the music went blaring by supper time I told him someone is going to call the Police and you're in trouble. Sure enough,

By 7 pm the Police dept came to the door and I ran in told him the cops want to talk to you outside. He said, "If you let them in the house I will kill you I swear on that boy's life." I went the door and opened up the curtain and told the cops I will turn it down and then as I said that Jack bolted out into the kitchen gave the finger to the cops through the curtain and said if any Police try to come through this door I will blow them away. That was it he just hung himself good. After 1 hour Jack went back to the window because the Police were getting ready to come in. He said, "If I come out to talk am I going to get arrested?" They said we just want to talk. He lit up a cig he knew he was going to jail and so did I, happy wasn't even close to the feeling I felt but, I knew mama would bail him out within hours.

The Police said would you like a protection order to keep him away I just laughed and said no that's just a piece of paper that's not going to stop him. Plus, his mom owns this house until I pay her off. I bought that house, I worked for that house and she wasn't getting it period. Well about 11 pm I heard a car coming up the driveway and sure enough the one phone call he made got him out on $2500 dollars bail and mama made it happen.

When he went to court he had 2 choices. Jail for threatening a Police officer for 3 months or, 3 years probation he took the probation thank god. Because you see I actually had some protection now if he got in trouble even for music he was going to jail even if it was for 2 or 3 hours. So he came home, had a few drinks and went to bed. I emptied out the vodka left over down the sink and would always tell him he drank it. He then started hiding it before he went to bed.

The next day I had a 12 hour shift because 2 people called in so I took the hours I had to make up for time loss .Within 3-4 hours a very drunk and belligerent

Jack calls and my boss answered the phone because I was in a meeting. He interrupted the meeting because it was an emergency at home my son may have broken his arm. I was so scared and wondered if he done anything to him so I raced home

Unfortunately, I got my only speeding ticket ever when I explained to the officer that there is an emergency he didn't care. I took the ticket and headed home. Standing in the front door, drunk on the porch with no shirt on, smiling at me as I drove up. I ran in the house and he said, "Go down to the store I need some more booze." I asked, "You lied and had me leave work to get you another bottle of booze? He laughed and said, "Just go do it then get the fuck back to your boyfriends at work. I went down got his bottle and called my boss and said, "My son was fine, He fell so I went back in and finished the day." About 1 hour before I was to clock out Jack called and said, "Where the fuck are you? You fucking bitch get your fucking ass back home now or I am coming to get you." I had 3 people standing around me that heard every word that he said. The woman covered her mouth and the managers just hung their heads. I was so ashamed and embarrassed. My boss told me to go home and I did. The next day was my last. My boss informed me that he got a call from Jack and was told to stay the away from his wife if you know what's good for you. That job was gone. I tried to get back into antiques for extra money but as soon as I made it he was spending it. His friends would come over with pills every night. Jack was binging on booze again now but this time he was on probation. I told him I was fired because he threatened my boss. So, he started screaming at me telling me I was no good I couldn't hold a job down and, I was a useless bad wife and bad mom. I pretty much believed him. My confidence and self esteem were gone the day we got married. The music started cranking very loud and I didn't say anything. I knew the cops were going to come and hopefully he will get arrested. Sure enough 3 hours later Police were banging at the door. Jack decided he needed to try to talk his way out. Jack proceeded to the back door.

Chapter 16

Jack, in Trouble with the Law again

The police had been listening to the screaming and the name calling they decided to press charges against him for domestic abuse and immediately put a protection order for him to stay away from the house. So, I am thinking he's going to be in jail for a while. Thank you, God. 48 hours later at about 9 at night the basement door sounded like it got kicked open and sure enough he was out. 24 hour PO hold
The PO officer was charging him with violation of probation unless I dropped all charges well I couldn't the police said it was out of their hands now but, they felt inclined to press charges because of the history of violence.
Every day before the court case came up he would threaten me and tell me you better make sure you fucking lie when you get on the stand because if I get put away because of you when I get out your dead so is your fucking family. And that evil look just made me cringe but I knew he would go through with it.
The case came up and I told the DA, "I am not testifying for fear of my life." He explained that I could put him away for a long time. I said, "I'm sorry. I have no faith in your

justice system." So, he dropped all charges and the protection order was dismissed.

Why didn't I do it? Well here goes. The reason is because no matter how many times he got arrested he was out with slaps on the wrist by the courts. But, I knew it wasn't over by a long shot I also knew winter was coming antiques were not selling because most of the shops were closed.

I had to get a job. Jack had gone through all the money we had saved. So I called the supermarket and asked them if they were hiring they put me on hold and came back on the phone and asked if I could come in today for an interview. I was ecstatic I went down and was hired on the spot to start at $8.25 per hour.

I was happy but, then thought how long I would be able to do this job before he calls the store and threatens my bosses.

The next week I got a visit from CPS. They said they got a complaint from the police about abuse in the house. Jack told me not to let her in. She said, "If you don't let me in I will be back with the cops and an order signed by a judge to remove my son from the house until further investigations. Well, he was scared of the cops. They were out to get him now.

The CPS worker came in and asked to speak to me alone. of course I had to deny everything and she wasn't convinced so she said, "I am opening a case and I am going to talk to the child's doctor and the school." I signed the releases and, off she went.

2 weeks later she stopped by and I went outside and talked to her and she said, "We can help you." I said, "No you can't." She said, "I went the school and got a disturbing report that my first son, Jack jr was going to school stating daddy was drunk all day and he and his friends would all sit around the living room jerking off to porno movies and that Jack had been beating him and abusing him for year." He was 8 at the time. Well, I was floored but,

I also knew that Jack jr was very violent and, hitting me was a trait he picked up from dad. Both boys I had; were taught to spit on me call me names and put me down. I had a talk with Jack and Jack said, "Give him up. I don't want him. If you bring him back in this house I will kill him."

Because at the time the CPS worker came over she was with the Police and served me a jeopardy order taking custody of my son. Within the next few weeks Jacks anger got worse and I knew if my son was returned Jack would kill him. He said, "He would bury the little cocksucker outside." He called him that all the time.

I went to the CPS office and spoke to the worker and told her the story I said, "He would kill the child." I want to sign over full custody of my son to the state because he needs protection and I can't give it to him. So, we went to court and Jack had to be there to sign over all parental rights. He was half drunk anyway and, after he signed the papers he said, he had to go to the bathroom. We finished up the case. My son was safe and away from this animal.

Jack didn't care in the least now he wanted a dog so he looked in the paper and someone had pit bulls he had to have one. He was abusive in every way and when Max was 1 he tripped in a hole in the back yard and I had to take him to the vet. The surgery cost $900 and I payed it.

The vet was so mad at me when they took max in he had 96 BBs lodged deep in his skin several were infected she said, "Someone's been torturing this animal. I lied and said it may have been the neighbors' kid.

Chapter 30

Pregnant Again

About 2 months later I started getting sick in the morning I would pray, "Please God no. Don't let me be pregnant please." I missed my period and sure enough I was pregnant with my second son. I started working at my new job but, Jack was drunk every day at this point and I was lucky to get 3-4 hours of sleep every night. I was exhausted and stressed out but I had to get through this then 9 months later my second son Jacob was born.

Jack was just an awful person and he hated kids. He was so jealous even if I played with my son if at any time I was tickling or playing with him he'd say, "What the fuck you doing? Clean this fucking house now. He was sober and was jealous and nasty. He hated my son. Jack kept a low profile music down and stopped fighting for a while to let things cool off he didn't want CPS back at the house or the cops.

It didn't last. He started calling all these people he met in jail looking for drugs and found a cocaine dealer named Mike. Now he was spending the money. I would have to always show him the check stubs to prove how many hours and how much I was making it was a good thing I would cash my check and pay the bills before I handed him the money. I told him I sent out the mortgage out of my check. Didn't he get pissed. "I handle the money in this house not you." All you need to do is you cash your check and bring it home first.

So, I did and of course he spent the mortgage and his mother called. He blamed me telling her I blew the money. I couldn't believe it but, I was used to taking the blame for everything that went wrong. Always it was my fault so I would take the hit.

She called later that night. He had passed out and I told her about the pills and the coke and the drinking and, I said I could not stop him she made like she was a listening ear. She said, "We will get through this what else is going on?" I told her cops were here quite a bit. She said she would cover the mortgage I told her I would make the payment next week before I give him the check but he was going to be pissed.

She hung up and, the next night called Jack and told him everything I told her on the phone. I couldn't trust anyone she didn't believe me. Anyway, I went to work and I got a call from Jack telling me I had to leave work now.

The house was surrounded by the police and they were trying to get into the house. I told my boss I had an emergency and they told me to go home. As I arrived there were 4 police vehicles in my driveway. I approached the police and asked what the problem was. And that I was at work and was called home.

The police officer told me Jack had cranked up the music and apparently the new owners of the other side of the duplex were done with his music. They said they banged on the wall and told him to turn it down or the Police would be called. Jack banged back on the wall and told them if they bang again he was coming over and, would shove this shotgun up their asses and kill all you mother fuckers. This was in the report.

I apologized to the neighbors but they didn't want any part of it. I don't blame them. I knew there was no to reasoning with Jack. So I finally told the cops to back off and let me in my house and I will talk him out because I wanted to get in there and see if my son was okay.

I told the Police he is a liar he doesn't own a gun. They said it didn't matter he threatened their lives, he was going to jail. Jack opened the door when the police backed off but granted they weren't going anywhere. He was going to jail. Finally again I told Jack they wanted to talk.

Jack went out on the Porch and the sergeant went behind him and told me to go back in the house. He was going to jail. 2 police officers immediately emptied 2 cans of mace in his mouth and eyes. Jack couldn't see. He was yelling to me to call his mom and get a lawyer. The police wrestled him to the ground and off to jail he went.

Peace at last but I knew he would be out soon the justice system couldn't hold him the probation officer let him go violated him and when court came up everything was dismissed. That was the story of my life.

After the arrest Jack didn't much care anymore. He started making pity calls to mom and threatened to kill himself several times and begging her to take him back but she said no. Jack started doing coke steady trading for weed and pills and always found a way to find something. On the phone constantly and bringing people in the house.

I came home one day and, my 32 inch TV set that I just bought a year earlier was gone. Jack said he got an eight ball for it. I didn't even know what the hell that was. He said coke you fucking moron.

Christmas was coming around and I had no money. I could get a discount at the store so I was able to pick up toys now and then. So my son could unwrap a few gifts and he had 3 relatives in New York sending 4-5 boxes of clothes and toys so he made out okay.

Jack had to lay off the music playing. Every time he turned it up the cops came and as long as he didn't threaten them and turned the radio down they left. I thought; he is on probation and he is drinking. I guarantee he's going to test positive for coke and other narcotics. I kept my mouth shut.

Chapter 18
The New Roommate

Jack got introduced to a guy who was
addicted to crack and he needed a place to stay.
So Jack being the good guy decides to give this
crack addict a home with meals and no rent.
Pay with drugs and he could live there forever.
Well, my life took a turn it was tax season and I
filed the taxes got back $4000.00 enough for
Jack to get high. He and our new roommate
decided they were going to get rich he took
1500.00 with him gave this man Corey the keys
to my car and off they were to get crack rocks
in Massachusetts.

Corey was from there and knew tons of
crack dealers that could hook him up with a
large amount for 1500 dollars keep in mind
Jack hid the rest of my income tax on me and I
could not find it.

26 hours later. The car drove in the yard
and behind them was the Police who started
following them as they got off the highway, I
knew they had crack at least that's what they
went for so I believed this was it.

Crack carried several years sentence
and I could be free for a long time, so I thought.
Well first off I ran out of the house and asked
the Police what was wrong and he said I need
to go back into the house; that he believed there
were drugs in the car and the Police dogs were
on their way. I don't how the hell this happened
but Jack jumped out of the passenger's door
and said I need to go to the bathroom the
Policeman says ok,

Are you serious I know he's got the
drugs on him and I can't believe you are letting
him in the house without searching him the
officer said come right back out when you're
done. What a joke. Jack ran into the bathroom

emptied all the crack out of his pockets and
went back outside.

The officer asked Jacks permission to
search the car and Jack said sure of course all
the drugs were sitting at the bottom of the
washing machine with clothes on top he knew
the car was clean and Corey had no drugs on
him he just went to buy it.

About an hour later the cop gave up on
the search he didn't find anything so he left.
Corey and Jack ran into the house laughing and
now the party began. They stayed up talking for
2 Days smoking crack and drinking vodka and
when the crack was gone 48 hours later he took
the rest of the income tax return and headed
back to Mass this time with 2500 hundred
dollars.

Chapter 19

Jack and Corey's Business Plan

He was so out of control I was begging
him to not take the last of the money I told him
the crack was addicting and he was addicted.
He looked up and said, "Are you calling me a
junkie? you fuckin' crack whore just a note
never did it and would never try it . But, he got
his way and headed down the road.

I was fighting with him because I had to
be at work in 2 hours and he was getting ready
to head to Mass. to get some more crack. But,
this time it was different they were going to sell
half, get the money back and keep half for free
and then head back to Mass. and keep doing it
over and over.

He had a business plan and we were doomed. I asked him what am I going to do. I need to be in work in the morning and it didn't matter if my job was on the line or not. Nothing mattered.

At 11:00 O'clock at night; they were pumped up on the last of the crack he bought and, ready for more. Corey assured me they would be back by morning so I could go to work of course that was I lie.

I called in to work in the morning and I knew I was all done. This was the 4th time calling out So when Jack arrived home things were sour with him and Corey apparently Corey's friend screwed Jack and only gave Jack $1500 worth of crack and ran off with the money apparently they met the guy, Jack was handed paper bag. And the guy ran away. When Jack opened the bag he saw that he got robbed.

Jack stopped at the liquor store and picked up a fifth so, he could grow some balls to confront Corey. By the time they got to Maine he was wasted and they smoked crack all the way home. When they arrived I announced to Jack I lost my job because the car was not back in time.

Well Corey came up with a plan to pay Jack back for the bad drug deal. He said it was a foolproof plan; every day he would go to hospitals and get pain pills and he would give them to Jack until Jack believed he got his money back and get rich selling pills at the same time.

So, they made up. Now Corey was younger and he worked out at one time Jack was always following him around the house to make sure I wasn't talking to him and,

whenever Corey came back to the kitchen Jack
would say, "What the fuck did she say to you?"
I guess Jack heard things that were not said and
even though the truth was told that nobody said
a word he believed Corey and I were having
sex. In his twisted mind he convinced himself
that Corey and I were fucking.

Everyday Corey left to get pills he let
me have it. Chasing me around the house
telling me he saw me staring at his cock. I was
sick of it so one night; I made sure Corey could
hear every word I said. I yelled out if you're
that jealous that you think Corey and I are
fucking why the hell is he here? Jack threw his
hand over my mouth apparently Corey had no
idea how Jack felt. He knew Jack treated me
like shit but, kept his mouth shut.

Well, the next morning we got up.
Corey and his stuff were gone. Jack was
devastated; his pills his crack connection and
his buddy were gone. Corey had left a note
thanking him for a place to stay but, he was
headed back to Mass. for good. We never saw
him again.

I was blamed for this and we fought
many fights about it. He would call his family
up and say that he couldn't have any friends
because his wife was a slut. So, that was the
last time we saw Corey, but it didn't matter.
Jack was in and out of jail and bars and was
bringing home all types of people.

There were a lot of people that would
come to the door and say Jack told us there was
going to be a party that night. I told them all,
"You've got the wrong place."

Chapter 19

Another Lost Job

Finances started getting tight and I found a job working in a nursing home it was not great money but someone had to pay the bills and support him. For years it was always said that I was a fat lazy bitch that couldn't hold down a job.

Throughout the years he told me several times, "If I ever told anyone anything about the way he treated me; I'd be dead." My life and my son's life had been threatened so many that it became a weekly saying.

I got the job working 40 hours a week. Jack started having day parties. I was scheduled to leave work at 3:00 o'clock but my relief called in sick and it was mandatory that I stay. I asked my boss to call Jack to tell him. Jack was screaming, "You get your fucking ass home now." I said, "If I left I would be fired, that's it. As he insisted for me to leave; my boss got on the phone and said, "It's mandatory that she stay, or his wife would be fired.

I packed up my stuff and, home I went. As I headed home devastated about losing another job. I knew I had to do something or the house was gone and, his mom would own it. I talked to Jack about setting up at a flea market and he agreed. I packed a few things for the flea market and I ran into a dealer that said, "You've got great stuff where do you buy? At auctions? I said, "I had never been to one." And as he explained auctions I got excited. Maybe I could make the money for the bills this way. What a great idea.

Chapter 20

New Friends and Pedophiles

Jack was starting to drink again and
when i came home from work one day I found
one of his friends there. The kind of people
that Jack associated himself with were the kind
I consider the lowest of society. First there was
Carl who had 2 kids. A 13 year old girl and a 6
year old boy. I didn't like him. I told Jack, "I
don't want him around." Jack told me that this
was his fucking house and if I knew what was
good for me I would shut my mouth. This
friend, Carl and his Daughter came over quite
often. Every week Carl's son got Ritalin and,
Carl was selling them or trading them for
marijuana. Well Carl brought his Daughter to
my house. I asked her if she wanted a sandwich
or a drink. She said no; but, I have something
to say and, you can't tell anyone. I said,
"What's going on?" She said that her dad
would sell her to the neighbor up stairs every
week. She had to do things so her Dad would
get free smoke." Just a note; the fact that both
parents were mentally disabled they did know
right from wrong. I was stunned. She said,
"Don't say anything because I'll just deny
telling." I said, "Why? I can help make it stop."
She ended up leaving about a half hour later. I

went in to sit on the couch and told Jack what was going on. I said, "That I needed to call someone. Jack said, "Mind your own fucking business you stupid bitch." I did call the Police dept. in the town they lived in and, I called CPS and made a complaint something had to be done. The detective in charge of the case said he would go over and have a talk with them. I told him, "Maybe you should wait until she was at school and away from the house. They didn't listen. Well, time passed and I couldn't call the Police because then Jack would know I told but, I had to find out so I came up with the idea to find out what happened. Unfortunately, I didn't leave the house for 4 days. Finally I went to the store and stopped at a phone booth and called the Police and CPS. I hadn't seen Carl or Crystal. I wanted to find out if the girl was okay. The detective in charge said. "The complaint was unfounded." Which meant there was no evidence and the girl said I was a liar." Nothing ever happened. Carl didn't come around too much after that. Jack would call him every day inviting him to party just to get the Ritalin. When Jacks supply of Ritalin died up, of course Jack just drank more.

Then Jack started looking for long lost relatives. Probably at this point is when I found out how much violence and abuse of all types were in this family. First, Jacks cousin had just got out of the hospital supposedly for mental issues. Jack wanted to see him. Jack called him and invited him over to party.

I got chills when he walked into the house and knew there was something about him I didn't like. Jack was happy to see him and I would tell him I need to clean the kitchen while they caught up on lost years.

They drank and snorted pills for hours. During this party Jacks cousin proceeded to tell him why he went to the hospital. The reason he was in the hospital was because he raped his 6 year old daughter and pleaded insanity. The courts deemed he was insane and sentenced him to the state hospital until it was safe to let him out.

Well, I guess 6 months was the limit because he was returned to the streets while his daughter to this day still receives counseling. Jack knew all this and didn't care and I was not allowed to say anything because he is and always would be a forever registrant and he was not allowed to be near any child under the age of 18.

He was getting all kinds of prescriptions Zanax , Cylert which was a form of Ritalin same effects and, this was the new thing he would rather have pills than alcohol until they ran out. For months his cousin came around every day and at this point he was told he could stop over any time.

Most of the time he never knocked on the door he just walked in. When I confronted Jack and said he needs to knock he said, "My cousin is my family and you're not going to start fucking trouble with him.

One night they both got really wasted on snorting and Jacks cousin about floored me there had been a murder and rape of an 11 year old girl. It was about 10 miles from my house. Jacks cousin said, "I have never told anyone this before. I raped and killed that girl and somebody else went to prison for it." I was stunned I told him you need to go to the Police and tell them what happened he said he was not going to jail.

Now I tried for days to figure out why someone would claim the brutal rape and murder of a little girl, if they didn't do it, and I was to keep my mouth shut about all of it. Jacks cousin said, he would deny it and Jack said I will just tell them you're a fuckin' nut job, nobody's going to believe you. And not to mention that there was a man sent to prison for the murder.

So, I would just look like an idiot and besides who would believe me anyway every time I ever told anybody anything it was a lie. But as god as my witness these words came out of his mouth.

It didn't matter whoever he had coming over that was supplying drugs, they were more important than anyone else. I was a piece of shit. Jacks cousin, after months of hanging around met a girl and brought her over to meet his cousin she was divorced with 3 teenage girls from 12-15 and they were head over heels in love.

When he started spending more time with his girlfriend than family that's when the threats came. Now just a note when Jack didn't get his own way as far as people saying no to him he would threaten them by telling them if they didn't start bringing the pills over at least once a week then Jack was calling his doctor and tell them he was selling his meds and he would contact the Police and testify that he is selling prescription drugs.

This didn't shock me at all everyone he dealt with buying pills he would threaten if they said no. Meanwhile I was thinking night after night about that little girl I had to tell someone. And, another thing that scared me was that when Jacks cousin came over the 13 year old was with him alone. They acted like lovers. I was so sick to my stomach. Well, I started to make some calls without Jack knowing.

He and his cousin would take off for hours in my car on a pill hunt. So, the first call I made was to the Police dept. that charged the man in prison for the girl's murder. Their first response was, we got the man in prison. The second call I made was to CPS to tell them a sexual predator that has to register for life has now moved in with a lady and 3 teenage girls.

Finally someone listened to me. I gave the info that I had and within an hour CPS was at the ladies house. The 3rd call I made was to the girl's father to warn him that his girls may be getting touched or worse. He thanked me and as I remember the dad went to Gale's house and picked up all 3 girls. A jeopardy order went into effect and all the girls went to their dads.

Thank god and hopefully it's not too late. It was the 15 year old that admitted to having consensual sex. Jacks cousin came flying through the door screaming frantically saying he didn't want to go to jail. I said, "Well if you didn't touch the girls then you have nothing to worry about."

They both just stared at me and Jack said, "Get the fuck out of here you stupid bitch.

Why would you say that to my family? We will talk about this later."

The girl broke up with him 2 days later. Jacks cousin lost it. He snapped and when he did he looked like Jack; he was frantically running around the house screaming stuff that was nuts, he couldn't complete a sentence and was crying then laughing hysterically. I was really scared I told Jack get him out now or I am calling the Police. I am scared he was going to snap.

At that moment Jacks cousin ran into my bathroom, dragged the washing machine to block the door and locked himself in the bathroom. The next few hours were so scary. He was banging walls and screaming not making sense talking about suicide and murder rambling on for hours. I knocked on the door and said, if you don't come out I am calling the cops. At that moment it went dead silent, and then I heard the washing machine was being moved. Good it's over I hope he leaves while Jack was in the living room. Jack told me not to say anything to his cousin and that he would calm down. Ain't anybody going to call cops on my family. I heard the lock click on the bathroom door and the door swung open.

I was struck with shock and disbelief his cousin was standing in the bathroom doorway smiling, naked and had a handful of semen as he looked at me. He threw his hand towards the tub and it was everywhere he had been in there for hours and there was semen everywhere the mirrors the floor the shower. I ran into the living room and screamed at Jack telling him what his cousin is doing. He stood up and smacked me in the head and said you been in there looking at my cousins dick,

I proceeded to tell him he swung the door open. He didn't hear a word I said except me seeing his cousin naked. I could tell he was getting very angry all he kept saying is you couldn't help but look at his dick how could you, my own fucking family you fuckin' whore. He stood up from the couch he punched me on the left side of the head as I fell hard. He walked by spit in my face and said, "You fuckin' shame me in front of my family you fuckin' whore wait and see what happens later within 2 minutes later my son was 3 and came over and spit in my face just like daddy.

I was laying there crying and when I got up I went to the bathroom to clean up and wash off the spit off my face when. He told his cousin to get dressed and then he and his cousin went into the living room sat on the couch and started snorting pills like nothing ever happened. In the back of Jacks mind he had convinced himself that I was interested in his cousin's cock. I could tell every time he came out into the kitchen he would say you fuckin' whore, my own cousin. And he was saying this in front of my son.

My son learned bad language young and hitting me was a Daily thing with him. What was I going to do? Just tell him no? That didn't stop him I feared he was going to be violent towards me right from the beginning he has been hearing and watching the abuse and violence since the day he was born. Anyway, Jack was so messed up on pills he barely could walk but, he wasn't going to let me forget. Finally 6 hours later the cousin left and I knew I was in trouble

Chapter 21

Jack's Rage and a Call to 911

After he shut the door he turned and looked at me and said, "Come here you fucking whore." He grabbed me by the hair of my head and threw me up against my china closet which broke the pane on the left side; he threw me on the floor and I ran to the corner.

I said, "You touch me again and I am going to call the Police. Jack went back in the living room and snorted a couple more pills, came back out ripped his shirt off and said you're threatening me? You fucking whore." "Huh, I can't wait to tell my mother and sisters that I can't even have my family over because my fuckin' so called wife wants to suck their dicks."

Well little that he knew when he went into the living room to snort I took the phone on the floor put it behind me dialed 911and left the receiver on the floor I just knew he was going to hurt me real bad this time. 10 minutes later there was a bang at the door the Police were there. Thank God. Jack looked at me and said, "Did you fuckin' call them? I said, "No."

He ran into the living room to turn down the radio and I hurried up put the phone on the hook and back on the telephone stand just in time he did not see me. He looked at me and said, "Don't you say a fuckin' word to the cops if you know what's good for you." Well, Jack wouldn't open the door for the Police he talked through the window. Jack refused to open the door.

The Police said we need to speak to Shelby, could you send her out? He closed the curtain and said, "They want you. What the fuck they want you for? What are you fucking the cops too you fat ugly fucking whore?" Go out there and get rid of them now.

Well, I stood up and ran to the bathroom to wipe my tears and thought what am I going to do? He's not done with me yet. He came in the bathroom and said quietly, "Don't fuck with me bitch I can make your life a lot more miserable if you don't get rid of them. I will take the kid to New York and sell the house and you will be back on the fuckin' streets where I found you."

This was actually told to me all the time since the buying of the house. I went to the door and Jack basically pushed me outside the door and locked it quickly behind me. The Police put me in the cruiser and said, "We heard him on the phone and we had been listening 5 minutes before we knocked and he is going to jail." I said, if you take him to jail; I am dead and he's going to take my kid.

They proceeded to tell me they needed me to press charges. I said, for some reason, "I value my life even if this is how I've got to live." They just didn't understand I was scared. Finally the Police left and said the next time they would be taking him to jail.

At this time he was off probation about 3 months so no violations, I wanted to tell them but, I was too scared. They ended up leaving and I went back into the house. Jacks first words were how the fuck did you get rid of them by promising to suck their cocks? I told him I refused to press charges. He returned into the living room and started snorting some pills at this time. He had several people selling him pills so, he didn't run out much.

All night his cousin was on his mind and as he started to think more he started to get very angry. His face turned beat red and, he stood up and said, "I think I need to teach you a fucking lesson seeing your still a fucking whore after all these years." I was petrified he was furious.

He took off his shirt and I got up and ran out the back door. It was night time and he couldn't see where I went. He was screaming out the back door you fucking slut you get your fucking ass in this house now before I find you. I didn't move I was hiding in the trees in the back yard afraid for my life, crying and praying. He couldn't find me. It seemed like I was out there forever waiting for him to pass out.

After the last time he came out screaming, someone called the Police and all I saw were headlights and blue lights coming up the driveway. I don't know what happened I froze. I was too scared to move they went to knock on the door and no answer Jack saw them coming up the driveway turned the lights off and made like we were sleeping. The Police left and then the outside light came on I knew he wasn't sleeping.

He yelled out, "You better get in here and make me something to eat." He wanted to go to bed. Why I went in I don't know, why I thought it would be over, I don't know. The second I got in the house he smacked me across the head open handed and said, "I am fucking done with you. You are a whore; make me something to fuckin' eat now."

He went into the living room and called his mom and told her she's a whore she wants to fuck my family, my own cousin and, she could never be trusted she was a fucking pig. They sat on the phone for about an hour putting me down. I had heard it all before so I just went to the kitchen to cook.

He was starting to come down from his high so, I knew it was only a matter of time. I decided to drug him to make sure he slept. He had been up for 3 days snorting pills and I was exhausted after the cousin incident, cops and fighting. I put 2 sleeping tablets crushed up in his Potatoes and, he went out within an hour.

Chapter 22

Jack and his Mom Try to Evict Me

In the next weeks to come Jacks mom didn't speak to me anymore. I guess she believed her son. I was vacuuming the living room when I saw a car pull in. I yelled to Jack I thought it was one of his friends. Obviously I was wrong I waited for a knock and when I opened it the man handed me a 7 day eviction notice. I said, you're wrong this house is mine.

He said 7 days or the sheriffs coming and this is for only you and your son. Jack was fine. I was furious they were going to steal my house and throw me and my boy out. Jack was smiling the whole time, thanking the man.

I was not going to let that happen I mean yes she cosigned the loan but, I paid every month even sending her double payments which she stole half and said she paid it. I went to see a friend of mine and asked his advice. He told me to fight it I did. I had no lawyer so; my friend helped me set up a defense. Jack thought it was a joke he told me, "You ain't going to win. The fuckin' house is mine and the kid stays with me or nobody I ain't having him hear you call all your other fucking men daddy. You would you whore wouldn't you?"

It was a fight every night anyway this just added wood to the fire. Mama called every night and they would laugh about me being homeless. The car, even though it was in my name, he would wreck so I couldn't drive it. He had taken out parts before so I couldn't leave and only gave me the keys when he needed to go somewhere to pick up his so called friends.

I went to court 7 days later and told the judge my case he decided that there was enough doubt in the case that we needed a trial. So, we went back to court and with the help of the real estate agent and the previous owner's statements and other testimonies it was concluded that the house was mine. I cried instantly tears of joy of course.

The judge asked Jacks mom to stand up; Jack was not there so when Jacks mom who spent 5 thousand dollars on a lawyer to try to steal my house and make her son the only owner, the judge said, "You should hang your head down and be ashamed of yourself to want to lie and steal this woman's house and to throw your grandson into the streets is preposterous." "I am putting the house in Shelby's name alone."

He turned to me and said good luck young lady and I am sorry you had to go through this and I want to commend you on a job well done you did a great job. I said, "Thank you your honor." And, about danced out of the courtroom. Finally someone believed me and I won. I was on cloud nine until I got home I told Jack I won but didn't tell him that the house was under my name solely.

His mom called after she got home to New York and told Jack he owed her $5000 for her lawyer fees. I was just so warm inside for now I had won. The next days and months to come he was very mean to me calling me names hateful and hurtful names. Jack now started threatening me and threatening to burn the house down because it was his house, not mine.

Every night and day he was so nasty and even worse. His mom stopped calling so; I got the blame for wrecking his family life and stealing his house. In the coming months Jacks cousin stopped coming around which thrilled me but, then Jack started looking for his other so called friends.

Chapter 23

Jack's Friend Mick and Attempted Murder

He found one his name was Mick. Keep in mind I did not know these people but I soon found out. Mick came over and they were best drinking buddies. I knew instantly that Mick was scared but, he obeyed all of Jacks commands to run to the store get booze, go in the kitchen and make me a drink whatever it was, Mick did it.

Well, one day Jack called Mick and of course I had to drop everything and go pick this guy up. He walked in the house and took his coat off at the kitchen table and proceeded to the living room. Jack was half in the bag already and it was only 2:00 in the afternoon. The first question Jack asked Mick was did that stupid bitch say anything to you? Mick stated, "She did not even say hi.

I went into the kitchen and noticed a bunch of papers fell out of his coat and were lying on the floor. I don't know what possessed me to grab them and go in the bathroom but I did. It was a protective order for Mick to stay away from his son. The accusation was Mick's 4 year old son claimed that Daddy was doing things to him in the tub when mommy left.

I was floored. Another pedophile where the hell do these sick people come from? I called Jack into the kitchen and he made a fool out of me in front of this freak. Telling him that I was a nosy bitch and looked at his papers that fell out of the coat. The contents of the papers did not matter and were not even questioned Jack didn't care.

Well, that night the music was so loud I was getting a severe migraine. Jack was smashed along with his friend. I told Jack I had to go lay down. I knew he wasn't turning the music down; he never did. About 1 hour later I awoke to Jack standing at the edge of the bed.

He ripped the blankets off and said, "What the fuck are you doing sleeping?

Get the fuck up I want you to go pick up Mick's brother. I said, "My head hurts and I am really sick." Out of nowhere he leaped on the bed and sat on me doubled up his fist and said, "What the fuck did you say to me?" I thought I was done. I said, "Okay I will go get him." he jumped off the bed and went downstairs and I proceeded to go get Mick's brother.

First Mick's brother, Mark was gay which I have no problem with but, the plot behind going to get him was unbelievable. You see, Jack was a very hateful person and he hated everyone especially gays and colored. I knew something was up there always was. As the night preceded the 3 three continued to pound down straight vodka and I went to bed. I was awaked at about 5:30 am the next morning. I had got about 3 hours sleep. Jack was sitting on the edge of the bed laughing and said," I knew it fags burn a blue flame when you set them on fire.

My heart sank and I knew something terrible had happened. I went down stairs and there was Mick's brother lying on my kitchen floor. I couldn't believe what I saw, this sick animal made my 7 year old son go down the basement and get the lawnmower gas can and when he brought it up he told Mick to douse his brother with the gas I guess he did what he was told. Then he told this Mick to light a match and burn him.

I was sick Mark lay on the floor his back was burned so bad I could see his flesh from neck to the waist. I started crying and Jack said, "You fucking stupid bitch what the

fuck you crying for? He's a queer. He deserved
it. I looked at Jack and said, "I need to get him
to the hospital or he is going to die." Jack said,
"Good, if he does his brother will bury him in
the back yard. I knew Mark needed to get to the
hospital or he was going to die.

He was going into shock and Jack, still
drunk was trying to get him drunk all over
again while Mark said, "What happened to my
back it hurts?" Jack laughed and said, "You
fell into the bonfire last night you were so
drunk. Mark said, "I don't remember the fire."
Which; there was no bonfire.

Well, I had enough; Mark started
passing out at the table and I pulled Jack aside I
said I am taking him to the hospital and get him
some help. If he dies someone's going to
prison. He smacked me across the face then
looked at me and said, "You want to fuck him
don't you? Well he likes cock you stupid
whore." I said get him into the car.

My head hurt so much but, this was it. I
knew after I got back from the hospital I would
pay for my deeds. I went to the hospital and
drove into the emergency room entrance and
ran into the emergency room and said,
"Someone help me I have a severely burned
man in my car 3 nurses came out with a
wheelchair and got him into the hospital. They
asked me to stay but, I split saying I don't
know him.

I knew in my mind I had to tell
someone because I knew if Jack was capable of
this monster act he would kill me. No doubt in
my mind. Never has been any. I got back home
and Jack was laughing about burning a blue
flame. He stood up and said, "What the fuck
did you say to the hospital? Did you fucking

lie?" I said, "I just dropped him off and I did believe the Police were going to get involved because the nurse said call the Police."

Jack was not scared. He said he didn't do anything. Mark's brother did it. 2 days later Jack had Mick called his brother at the hospital. Not to see how he was doing but, to make sure the story was straight. Jack wanted Mark to say it was the bonfire accident. Then Jack got on the phone and said, "If you tell the Police anything other than that story; next time I will fuckin' bury you in my yard and nobody will care."

I could not believe this. He threatened the man's life if Mark didn't say what Jack wanted. When Jack got off the phone he said I don't think he's going to talk after I spoke to him. They continued to drink and about 3 hours later a Police officer came up to my back door and was knocking on it. Jack immediately looked at me and said, "Don't fuck with me bitch you better get them to close the fuckin' case. I mean it."

I went out the back door and spoke to the Police officer. He said, "Did you see what happened last night?" I said, "No but I took him to the hospital." The officer said, "Mark claimed he fell into the bonfire." I said, "Maybe you should look into it further."

He said that he was just finishing up and was closing the case. I was shocked. He said he had a statement from Mark that he fell into a fire being drunk. The case was closed. Jack got away with it. Mark was transported to the Boston burn hospital where he stayed for 3 months. We never saw him again. Mick disappeared after that. I was to blame for his

friends not coming around and I was driving
them away.

With no one else to torture, it was back
to me. The next few months were hell I was a
slut that couldn't be trusted that's why he
couldn't have friends around me. For a while,
he had no pills. He got so sick from coming
down off them he couldn't do it and had to
have booze. He always said to me; he had to
have something in order to live with me.

I really could not believe nothing
happened to them but then again it was the
story of my life.

Chapter 24

Jack's Friend Jason

Within the months to come the situation
got worse; Jack was on probation and he met
up with an old friend Jason who was in to drugs
bad and just got his kids taken away for abuse
and neglect. Because he kncw where to get
drugs he was awesome to Jack. Well, one Day
Jack and Jason decided to go to a contact of
Jason's to score some cocaine and they were
both drinking vodka.

I prayed they got stopped and arrested,
one of the conditions for Jacks probation was
no drugs or alcohol. I knew they were drunk
and were going to get drugs. I should have
made a call to the Police but, I had no idea
where they went they would not tell me.

About 3 hours later they pulled up in
my car and staggered out into the yard, Both

were smashed, now. Keep in mind Jack did all the coke buying and Jason had no money. So, they had a fight in the back yard. When I went out Jason started walking down the driveway and looked at Jack and said, "You sure you want to do this?"

I didn't know what they were fighting for and I didn't care. Jack screamed at the top of his lungs, "You wanna fuck with me? I'll fuckin' bury you. Jason was gone when Jack came in the house. He was fired up. I knew if he couldn't find anyone to fight or hang out with I was in for a long night. So, while Jack was telling me that Jason wanted half of the eight ball that was purchased or he was going to the cops and turn him in for drinking and drugs.

I was praying and kept looking out the window all night long praying for the blues. They never came that night. But, the next Day, I woke up to a banging on the door I knew it was cops because they always knock very loud. Jack didn't want me to open the door because he thought Jason had turned him in.

But here's what happened when Jack and Jason took off. After they got the coke I guess within minutes of leaving his dealers house they got into a fight while Jason was driving. I guess they were swerving in and out of traffic. A state trooper pulled them over and when the trooper was getting ready to get out of the car Jason turned to Jack and said I want 1/2 the coke when we get back to you house or I'm telling this trooper your loaded with cocaine so Jack agreed. The trooper asked their names and they explained that they had an argument but everything was fine now. The trooper said, "What are your names?" Jack lied and gave his

dead fathers name. Big mistake. First of all
again he violated probation no lying to Police
about name or address.

He knew if he had given his real name
he would be arrested for drinking and they
would find the coke. Well, Jack told me this
and said make like we are not home but, the
Police weren't going anywhere they were
stationed in my back yard waiting for him to
come out.

Chapter 25

Jack in trouble with the Law Escaping
to New York

We had an attic with no windows and
we were forced to live in this crawlspace that
night. It was horrendous about 95 degrees and
breathing in insulation that was exposed
everywhere. Finally, the Police left and I didn't
expect the next rendezvous, we were headed to
New York.

Jack wouldn't let me get any shoes on
my feet nothing. He wanted out. The cops were
coming back and he knew he was going to jail.
This was his 5th violation on this probation. So,
midnight came and off we went. I hadn't slept
in days and I was so scared we didn't have
directions.

Jack said we'll stop and get directions.
Wow, so we hop in the car and head out after
being lost for hours I finally found his mom's
place I did not want to be there but keep in
mind he was in control of everything the

money the car keys everything. So, I couldn't just get up and go when I wanted.

When we arrived in New York it was 11am and I was so tired. The first thing his mom said was you can stay but, her and the kid have got to go. We weren't welcome there. Believe me that was fine I had no problem I wanted to drop him off but, I asked her what can I do? I have no money to get home and haven't slept in 40 hours.

I was so exhausted. She agreed to let me get some rest but, wanted me gone. She would give me the gas money. I was so happy for a second, what was I stupid? He's not going to let me go. I was right. In the next few days I was treated like shit. Everywhere I sat down she sprayed air freshener.

I shower every day she was just being an idiot and trying to belittle me but, they were both the same. They loved to laugh at me and put me down. I used to cry for hours now my sadness was becoming angry. I was done I looked at her 2 days later and said I hate you. You are the nastiest bitch I have ever met.

I wanted her to throw me out at that point I was worried whether or not they would let me take my son. She had already retracted the idea of giving me money for gas. That was not happening. So she left to go to the store and said if she and the kid are not gone by the time I get back she was calling the police and telling them you are on the run from Maine. Then she left.

Jack was pissed he threw me on the floor and said, "So you see what you fucking did you nasty bitch you fucked everything up. Now we've got to leave." I asked him, "Why don't you let me and my son go back?" We still had a house to take care of. At first I thought he agreed to it but, when his mother came home he did a little pity routine telling her the plan was to leave him in New York and take the house.

She said, "I want her gone now." As she picked up the phone Jack ran up to her and shoved her into the staircase and said to me, let's get the fuck out of here. We drove for about 1/2 hour and stopped by a phone booth He called his mother and started crying like a baby; begging her to at least let him back and he would give me the gas money to get home.

She said it's too late you better get out of New York the cops have your license plate number. He screamed for another 30 seconds, hung up and said, "Let's get the fuck out of here, the bitch called the cops but, don't worry I will get her back.

Chapter 26

Shelby is Sick from Stress

He did not want to go back to Maine the Police were looking for him and he was facing a year in prison. So, his brilliant idea was we go back to Maine, stay at a campsite 50 miles from the house and look for a place to live. The stress was taking a toll on me and I started bleeding internally.

I threw up all blood 2 times and told Jack I need to go to the hospital. There is something wrong I showed him where I threw up and he said it was something you ate. I started to double up with pain and I guess Jack was afraid I would die; only because he had no driver's license, and still had a warrant out for his arrest. He finally let me go to the E.R. and they ran some test and said, I had to stay in the hospital.

I was bleeding internally and they had to remove the blood in my stomach and find out what was causing the problem. I knew Jack was not going to let me stay no way. I told the doctor I couldn't I needed to go back to the house and let my husband know what was going on. They did not want me to leave and kept saying you will die if we don't stop the bleeding. I promised them I would be back explaining to the nurse that I was the only licensed driver. I needed to make sure my son had everything he needed. They agreed but I had to sign myself out.

When I got back to the campground Jack was wild I had been gone for 3 hours and he was low on vodka. I told him what was going on and instantly he told me I was a liar and said I was not going anywhere. I told him it was a matter of life and death he laughed at me and said you're a liar. Finally, he agreed after screaming for hours I was in too much pain and it was hard to even stand up.

He said I could go on 2 conditions I was to buy him a gallon of vodka and wasn't allowed to stay the night. They had to do everything in one day. I knew we were going to have problems. I did as I was told. I got food and vodka and headed back to the hospital and gave Jack the number to the hospital so he could check on me and make sure I was there.

When I arrived they were happy to see me and admitted me right off. I told them I have a problem and I needed to be out of there by the end of the night they said that's not happening because they had tests to do and they scheduled the surgery the next morning.

Well, 2 hours later Jack got through to my room from the campground. There was a phone booth there. He was drunk and started screaming at me. In my room were 2 nurses, a doctor, and an anesthesiologist and they all could hear Jack screaming and telling me I better get back he wasn't taking care of no fucking kid all night.

The doctor grabbed the phone covered the mouth piece and asked politely what is your husband's name? I said Jack. The doctor got on the phone and said, Is this Jack? Jack asked, "Who the fuck is this? He said I am the doctor that is going to operate on your wife tomorrow morning." Jack said, she is signing herself out put her back on the phone. He didn't he looked up and said; this is how it's going to go Jack. Your wife is staying overnight and getting this surgery done and if you make her leave and sign herself out before she gets this done I will see to it personally that you're charged with murder. I am going to hand the phone back to your wife. When the phone came back to me Jack said, "Who the fuck is that quack?" I said what do you want me to do? He said stay but you better be back in the morning after your surgery.

The next morning was surgery and they found out I had a hole in my stomach lining they did what they had to do and when I woke up one of the nurses said Jack had called 50 times in 2 hours. Omg she said he was so nasty to them and she asked if I was going to be okay going back home with him. I wanted to say no,

I am not safe. Never have been safe with him. But instead I said I would be fine. He doesn't like to be alone.

I left a few hours later. While I was gone he made friends with a guy and his wife that were camping at the same site. I didn't like the looks of them, because he was a drinker and he was so mean to his kid and old lady. The two started staying up late at night with bonfires and booze.

One night Jack was screaming at the top of his lungs fighting with me telling me it was all my fault he that had to live this way and going on and on for hours the guy screamed out hey we're trying to sleep. Could you keep it down? Jack said fuck you, why don't you come over and make me. The guy packed up instantly and left.

Chapter 27

Kicked Out of the Campground

The next morning the owner of the campground said we needed to leave and never come back. And we did. I got the paper and started looking for a place the further away the better. I found a place. A 2 bedroom trailer far enough away from my house but only an hour away from there. I had to get to the place drop, Jack and my son off and get loads of stuff for the trailer. I moved what I could and had no help with anything and all I got when I returned with a full load; Jack was screaming and yelling saying I took too long and I must have stopped in to see a few of the men I was fucking back home. I was tired and prayed this couldn't last too much longer hopefully on one of my moving trips a cop would notice me and pull me over or follow me. But no, that didn't happen.

I knew I also needed to get a job we needed money to live and he was spending what we had on booze. Summer was ending and a year had gone by. The violence grew worse and the hitting got harder I finally found a job and he had to stop hitting me because I couldn't go to work with bruises on my face so he used words, nasty hateful words every day and night. So, that year which had made 2 years in this trailer my son turned 6 and guess what; school was in session and I knew that would give away the location and he would get arrested.

In the meantime he made up with his mama. I registered my son in school, and started my job working at a bank.

The bank I worked for had a program that would pay my mother in law in full all my debts and the house would be paid off with her. I qualified and did not tell them anything until the paperwork went through now the mortgage company had no problem with the loan except one condition was to pay off everything on my credit report.

I was okay with that. Jack had 11 thousand in credit card bills racked up in my name and I wanted to clean it up. When I got the call that it was approved it was solely in my name. The loan and the house. I was so happy. Jacks mom was thrilled to get her 8 grand I owed her for the house but Jack wasn't happy. Why the fuck should he have to pay all the credit card bills he wanted that money himself. So he and his mom tried to think of ways they could lie and say I owed Jacks mom 15 thousand instead of 8. Too late the checks were on the way to her and all my debtors.

I was happy about this but, things didn't get any better he was accusing me of affairs at work and every day I would go through hell. I was praying that soon this would end .Well, the loan came through and of course I again was the talk of the family. First of all everything I did had nothing to do with them. Well it was very hard for Jack to get drugs or pills because he knew nobody.

He told me to snoop around at the bank. There had to be someone that sells drugs. Was he serious? Wow, I could not believe it but by this time we had been married 18 years.

Chapter 28

Shelby's Chance to be Free

I wanted out and I got my chance while I was doing an antiques show apparently the cable went out and my 6 yr old son called 911 to tell them they need to fix the TV he was watching SpongeBob and was missing the show then hung up. The Police of course thought the child was home alone but daddy was passed out.

The Police broke the door down and searched the trailer but didn't find anything. While the Police were searching, the 2 of them piled all the clothes in the closet on top of them to cover them up. This made Jack scared. Apparently the Police waited and weren't satisfied.

They came back to the house 2 hours later and found Jack by hearing him yelling at the child. Immediately they announced at the door who they were and just came in and arrested him. DHS was notified and the child was sent away.

I came back 3 hours later and when I found out what happened I was so scared for my son I didn't know where he was and the Police wouldn't tell me where my son was just that he was taken. I was sick I couldn't go to work I cried so much and couldn't sleep, couldn't eat it took me 5 days before someone came to my house and told me where my son was.

They said because you left your son in a dangerous situation where the dad had a warrant out for his arrest and a history of violence they were placing my son in foster care. I was stunned I was scared I didn't know what to do. But the guardian ad litem said divorce Jack and we will give the child back to you. I said yes, yes, yes. Well, Jack spent 3 weeks in jail and was given time served with the agreement that he stayed on probation 3 more years.

I did not care this was the chance God gave me to go, and I took it. But, it wasn't easy to get rid of Jack; not by a long shot. First thing I did and I got to tell you I was scared and happy for the first time in my life when I walked in that jail and handed the bailiff the papers.

       I wanted to see him and tell him face to face. I sat in the jail and waited for the guards to bring him in. I loved the window between us it meant he couldn't touch me. I told him first that the DHS had my son and I needed to get a divorce in order to get him back. Jack said okay I will agree to divorce if afterward we get remarried and we move to New York after the house was sold. I said okay knowing this was never going to happen. I was done and I will be free of him even if it killed me.

       Jack got out with time served. But with his mothers money she paid for a quick release. I have got to say I have no faith in the justice system and never will. I got a call the day he was released this is the voice I never wanted to hear again but, knew it was going to happen. Jack signed the divorce paper in the jail which I was so happy about; the only thing was the dividing of the real estate and the antiques. I went into this divorce alone no lawyer nothing he had a 5000 dollar lawyer the first day of the trial it got dirty and the judge recessed for lunch.

       Jack ran out and said I need to talk. I said never alone again I want a Police officer. He said you're fucking nuts you are my wife. I said NO MORE, NEVER AGAIN! What a relief. A great weight lifted from me I couldn't believe I stood up to him of course his lawyer was there and said if you give up the house and the antiques we will give you the child.

I stood up and could not believe what I said. I said buddy you are probably a good lawyer so you might want to recommend to your client that if we go back into that courtroom with the request you want. I will tell the truth. Jack said what truth what are you talking about? I said I will the courts everything.

Jack knew what I was talking about when I mentioned Mick's brother that you severely scarred for the rest of his life. I said not only will I mention this to the judge but also how you treated me throwing me outside in the winter nude 2 times and honey it won't stop there. I will tell them everything. He hung his head down and said what do you want to do? I said, "I will fix the house and after the repairs I will get reimbursed for, it will be sold and the balance will be split in half. I will split the antiques up and bring you all your personal stuff of course with a Police escort and as far as the child is concerned the DHS will decide what you need to do to see him.

He knew he had no choice and said okay. I was so surprised that after the deal I went to the ladies room and quietly burst into tears. It was almost over, this hell. Not even close. I had lost my job at the bank and had no income.

I rented a room until I could find a job and my own place. Within the days to come I had to situate everything and divide the stuff and bring it there to his mother's house. So I contacted the Police and asked for an escort. I will never trust him again. The Police said sure when you get into town just call them and when I finally arrived about 1/2 mile from his mother's house, I called the Police and said I

was needing an escort just to unload the stuff
and I feared for my life. The dispatcher
apologized to me saying all officers were on
call nobody is available.

Chapter 29

It's Finally Over! Maybe

     Great, a carload of stuff and I had to
give him what the judge ordered .It was court
appointed and I was on the last day of the
deadline. If I didn't get the stuff to him I would
be in contempt. I called Jacks mom and told her
to open the garage. I would unload the stuff in
there.
     I really believe that Jack and his mother
had a plan to get us back together but, I had
made up my mind IT'S OVER!!! I pulled in
mom's driveway and immediately she said,
"Oh Shelby could you stay for supper I made
spaghetti." I said, "No thanks." For real, I was
treated like a piece of garbage by her and him
for nearly 20 years. It just amazed me how bad
they wanted us to get back together.
     I unloaded all the stuff and told Jack I
would have the rest the next day. He said,
"When are you coming back to me?" I said,
"Never." He said, "You found another cock
right?" and started blocking me from leaving he
grabbed my breast and he said, "You are mine
forever the marriage was just a piece of paper."
     I blew up and said, "Get your hands off
me. You will never touch me again ever on my
sons life I swear I will never let you touch me

again. I hate you. You have no idea how much." I know hate is a strong word but I meant it. I ran out of the house he came after me and started to pull me out of the driver's seat. I slammed the car in reverse and he flew backwards. I stepped on the gas and he was yelling in the streets; you fucking whore I will kill you.

Apparently he could not take the rejection. That's when he started threatening me on the phone, telling me he owns me. I would ask him, "Does your probation officer know your drunk right now?" and he would hang up. But it didn't stop and for some reason I believe he never will let go. And he won't stop until he or I die. Months went by and I had so many fears in me that I went to see an abuse counselor. I didn't tell her everything but I told her quite a bit. She said it was the most horrendous case she ever heard and said I should write a book to give hope to all the abused women out there. I pondered the idea at the time but never did anything until now. The divorce was final. It took 6 month but it was final. Thank god for finally answering my prayers. Within the months to come I was threatened and the people I was staying with were threatened by Jack, burning the house down with everyone in it, Stabbing me and making sure I was dead, or disfiguring me by carving my face so no guy would ever want me. These were serious threats so I saved all the messages and went to the Police I was afraid he would carry through with them. I played the evidence to the officer and he said that he would call Jack and tell him one more call and he will be arrested. This worked for 2 weeks and I guess the drink got to him after a while it was too much. Jack and his mom called the DHS and said I was snorting pills and doing all kinds of drugs and that they believed my son was being touched. I really couldn't believe that both of them would do this. I invited DHS into the place I lived in and they said we apologize. I said I know you can't tell me who did this but, I know because they told me they called. DHS closed the case urging me to get a protection from abuse order from Jack. I said I would but, you know like I said I had no faith in the justice system which failed me so many times. Of course the Police take it a little more serious now because women have died because of people like Jack who continues to stalk me. But in the meantime I had a problem. My son was returned to me but I didn't want to bring him to see this animal oh my god I just knew that it was going to be bad. Well I guess I had no right to keep him from his father because it did not matter that I was tortured for 20 years. It didn't matter that he was abusive. I got away with it for 1 year keeping my son from him and I changed my phone number. In the meantime I found out that Jack was bettering himself through AA and therapy. I'm sorry, there is no help. He's not going to change I know. Well here it came subpoenaed to court charged with possible contempt of court because I agreed in court to visitations. I had no choice they had lawyers and I didn't. The day came; I went to court alone I couldn't get anyone to go into court with me and I was really scared of losing my son.

Chapter 30

A Custody Battle

The judge was very mad at me and said
I have a choice, bring my son to his father's
every Friday and pick him up Sundays every
week for visits or I would be held in contempt
for violating a court order. Of course you know
if I was jailed he would get my son for sure. I
agreed but I need help with gas money he
should pay that and no drinking or drugs there
at the time of visit. The judge said okay he pays
half of the gas. I've never seen a nickel; He
always said next month he would catch up.

Of course he used my son by calling me
50 times a day saying our son is crying every
night because he wants to live with his dad and
he didn't want to live with me anymore. I knew
he really did but what happened after really
blew me away. After 2 months I told him if you
don't stop calling me and start paying for the
gas we are going back to court what he did was
hang up the phone, 3 hours later Jack called. He
was drunk and furious.

He said his son has something he wants
to tell you my son got on the phone and said I
want to live with daddy. You are a whore and I
hate you. I said, "I am on my way to get you."
It was Friday. I told Jack he will come home
with me tonight or I will make sure you go to
jail tonight.

We will be back in court and this time I
will get a lawyer and the truth will come out on
the stand. Everything, and when I am done
telling the truth you will never be able to see
your son but tonight I am coming for him with
or without the Police.

He started crying and said, "Please don't take my son from me he's all I got that is a part of us." I can't have you no more at least give me my son. I said go to bed and call me tomorrow you are drunk. My son got on the phone crying saying please mama let me stay. I will tell you if he drinks tomorrow I promise.

My mind was going crazy right now I really didn't know what to do the rest of the night was quiet no more calls. The next morning I got up to a phone call from Jack's mom, Jack was arrested last night and I needed to come get my son. Oh yes I was so happy. I hopped in the car and drove to go get my son as I pulled in the driveway they were outside waiting and my son was bawling.

I was trying hard not to cry but I couldn't help it he kept saying is daddy getting out soon? Am I going to see him? Over and over. My son is autistic but could talk well enough. He just messed up some words but, I understood him clearly. I finally got him calmed down by taking him to the burger place. And ice cream on the ride home. Now, every time he gets back from his dads he is abusive and very violent but it was all talk and I knew he's just a boy.

Chapter 31

Shelby and Jack's Son
	Becomes very violent

I could restrain him if he starts doing anything to hurt himself or anyone else. Well, first it was cups flying, throwing chairs on the floor and running out and slamming the door telling me he going to his dad's. I knew he wasn't because he understood that dad violated probation and had to serve 18 months in prison.

Hopefully in that period of time I could get my son away from his dad and he wouldn't be violent and calling me names.

But, as I stated earlier my son is autistic and so repetitive with words and behavior. It was a daily thing for him. When he got something in his head he could not let go. Being with dad was all he wanted. He didn't want to live with me.

It didn't matter he was getting stronger and he hurt me when he slapped me in the face and it was happening so many times and out of the blue come into the kitchen smiling take 5 steps toward me and slap me in the face saying dad said you're a whore.

I fell into a deep depression. I had no where or no one to turn to my son not only was threatening to slice my throat but do it when I was sleeping. I had no choice I called the Police. The Police came over and asked what was wrong the officer was well aware of my sons violence so he asked my son what's going on. He told the officer straight out I am going to slice my mother's throat and everyone else's tonight with a very evil grin looking exactly like his dad very cold and not there mentally.

Then he went towards the cop and reached for his gun. They had him transported to the hospital for evaluation and med changes this went on so many times while Jack was in jail. When Jack got out of jail my son was in the hospital and I did not want him to have permission to go see him.

Jack was the reason I was going through this because he brainwashed and took advantage of a precious little gift that was given to me.

I love children I really do. My son was released from the hospital he secretly called his dads number from my apt. which I had changed before Jack got out of jail and now he was back on the kick of violence calling me names and physically hurting me. I was restraining him on a daily basis he was getting suspended from school constantly, the Police were called by the school for him running around the classroom with a pair of scissors threatening students.

I was able to calm him down and he was suspended indefinitely and the school would provide tutoring which he abused 2 of his tutors the school system gave up on him he was too violent he was starting to treat me like his dad did, it was really scary.

I did not want to start the visits again but I had no choice he was getting bigger and stronger and one day he struck the young girl across the face with his fist. I was done I'm sorry I can't do it I called DHS and had a case worker over and told him what was happening well my son came home and immediately said I want to go to my dad's it was Monday I said Friday I have to bring you. You have school till Friday. He immediately threatened to kill me and he smiled at the worker and said I wish she was dead I am going to stab her.

I looked at the worker and said I can't sleep I want him hospitalized now or I am handing custody to you so you can get him help one way or another he asked about relatives and my son wasn't allowed around kids or babies because he was threatening to kill them almost all of them were under the age of 4.

So DHS took custody and hospitalized my son. I was not allowed to go see him at the hospital as he was extremely violent and attacked several kids and adults on the unit it wasn't safe 2 weeks passed. My son was released but nobody would tell me where he was.

About 1 week later I get a call from my son I said where are you? He said I am at my dad's house. Jack got on the phone and said the state gave him temporary custody of my son and charged me with abandonment. In the meantime mama paid for the same lawyer and now we were back in court and Jack was seeking full custody because he wanted to start collecting the disability check.

Chapter 32

Jack gets Custody

At the courthouse as we were waiting for the case to be heard my son wouldn't look at me. His dad said go give your mother a hug he said that's not my mother and I don't love her. It broke my heart but I stood up and said I will give you full custody and sign off rights but DHS will be involved and I will make sure you are drug tested a lot but, I am going to explain my son's medical issues and diagnoses to the judge before he makes his decisions.

When we got into the courtroom I explained to the judge that my son is not mentally capable of making a life decisions he is autistic, high functioning and he needs to be hospitalized. He is very violent he is going to either hurt himself or someone else.

The judge wanted to hear my son talk so in judges chamber he went after 15 minutes we were called back in the court the judge called my son on the stand and swore him in and he asked my son if he knew what that meant and my son said, "Yes if you lie after you swore on the bible you were going to hell and be in big trouble. I always smile thinking about this.

The judge asked him where do you want to live? He said, "With my dad I love my dad very much and I do not want to live with my mother. I don't love my mother. The judge said the child knows where he wants to live it is my judgment that Jack gets custody and visits will be setup for the mother.

I knew he was getting full control. My heart started hurting I couldn't breathe tears just started pouring down. I lost my son forever but, I knew that the DHS was staying involved. Jack was still on probation and if he called me and I knew he was drunk I would call his probation officer and I will make sure my son does not ever live with Jack.

Within the first week he was having my son call me and then rip the phone out of his hand and say let me talk to her. I told him I want to talk to my son not to you. He would said, I am the one who decides who he can talk to. Control, he thought he still had control and he was obsessed. He really thought that he was going to get me back that I would crumble but I didn't. So, when he realized I didn't want to speak to him he turned the tables on me. The calls started coming in. First my son would call and I knew he was being coaxed on the phone because he never talked to me like that he said you're a fuckin' whore and I hate you and I wish you were dead. Then Jack would get on the phone and say I am sorry he's fuckin' talking to you like that. I'll talk to him later, I said, "Put him back on the phone." Jack said, "He's in the bathroom." My son said, "I'm right here. Can I talk to my mother? Jack said, "Go brush your teeth." I said, "I am hanging up. When my son can call me and talk to me I will talk to him."

That pissed off Jack. So, as Jack got drunker the nasty phone calls were all night he kept that boy up all night calling me and saying, "You're a whore and I hate you. I wish you were dead." So, stick it up your ass bitch I heard dad in the background word for word. It took a lot for me to say no more. I changed my number it was a hard decision to make but I had no choice. I had a lifetime abuser I was dealing with and now he is having my son say the nastiest things to me.

I knew my son would never talk to me like that if his dad wasn't involved at least he didn't before. I knew it was coming because it's in his genes; the violence the explosive violence. I did call the DHS and told them about the calls and that I didn't think my son was safe.

They needed to go check on him. They went once and that was the first week he had custody and then they dropped the case. I guess Jack and his mom put on a hell of a show. Oh yes, I forgot to mention: Jack will always live with his mom. He can't live alone he has to have someone around.

Chapter 33

Jack goes back to Jail

Well, within the next few months I got a letter in the mail from the county jail, it was Jack. He was arrested, 1 month ago for putting his 76 year old mother in the hospital. She wanted him to quit drinking and get help or move out. Well, Jack apparently punched her in the stomach and threw her against the stove and the ambulance had to be called.

Jack was arrested and my son was put in foster care. But, within days my son was brought to the hospital for slapping the foster mother and pulling a knife on them. So in this letter he said the state agreed to give Jack back his son after he gets out of jail and completes anger management, and AA classes.

I never wrote back. I got a call from DHS. They said they wanted me to take my son back because they have tried to place him but he gets so violent and ends up hurting people. I said I'm sorry I am in Poor health and I can't restrain him anymore he is too strong.

They gave custody back to Jack on the condition that Jack move out of his mother's house and sign up for mental health services for both my son and himself. That lasted about 6 months. I got a call from the Police department there was so much screaming in the background.

My son was crying and yelling and I guess the Police officer went outside and this is what the lady officer said to me. We have a situation; your son needs a place to stay. I said I am sorry I dont have custody there's nothing I can do. The officer said what kind of mother are you to where you can't come and get your son? And then hung up.

I was so mad. The nerve; what gives her the right to say that? I called her boss the next day and they said they would look into it. I never heard anything back.

Now here's what happened. Jack and my son who was now 16 were drinking all night. I guess after the phone call my son tried to grab the cop's gun and threatened to kill everyone. They handcuffed him and brought him to the hospital. He had to be sedated because he was so violent and his blood test revealed a high alcohol level. First of all, why didn't the cops arrest Jack for giving alcohol to a minor?

Apparently my son threatened to kill has father and pulled a knife on him and attacked his father stabbing him in the forearm. Jack had to be taken to the hospital for stitches. He ended up having the Police in my town come to my house and give me a message. I called and I forgot caller id. I would have to just change my number again.

So, this is Jacks side; he called me a liar about the alcohol and said my son was stealing it and getting drunk all the time while Jack was sleeping. I knew everything he said was a lie. I could not visit my son at the hospital but I just had to know that he was okay.

I went to the hospital and of course I couldn't see him the Police came out immediately to escort me out. So, I went home and called the hospital and I don't know what happened but I got my sons room my son picked up and I started crying. I said, "Are you okay, are you hurt?" he said, "I'm okay. I want to get out I want to go back to my dad's. I said well you have to wait a little while; the hospital needs to check you out.

I asked him if he stabbed his dad he said, "Mama I swear on the bible, after I threatened him with the knife Jack grabbed the knife and stabbed himself and said, "You little cocksucker now you're going to jail. Then he called the Police."

I said, "Well you need to listen to the doctor and try to get some sleep. He started talking crazy saying he was going to kill everyone on the floor. He said, "I feel like I want to kill someone right now." I started talking about music; and this was starting to calm him down.

Finally, a nurse came on and said who is this? I said, "His mom." She said, "You are not allowed to talk to him, nobody is." I said, "Chill out, I am trying to calm him down."

All I heard next was, "Hey, you need to get back in the room." Then click. Within the next few days or so, I just kept thinking about my son. I got a call from Jack and he said, "He just got out of the psychiatric ward and spent 48 hours in there." I didn't care they should have kept him. He said he told the doctors he stabbed himself so the Police wouldn't charge my son and had to stay 2 nights in the hospital. He said, "If I ever told anyone he would hunt me down."

He wasn't going to lose my son and his check because the apt. he was in had nothing left out of his check. "Wow, all you care about is the money." I said. "So, you're feeding him booze now huh?" He said, "You crazy fucking bitch he is stealing it from me." I said, "Lose this number or I will have you arrested. Don't call me anymore."

I didn't get a call for 6 months. Apparently, within this period of time Jack was going to counseling, the state gave him back my son and they moved back into his mother's house. Well, that didn't last long. Jack was still on probation and got drunk. This time he hurt his mom real bad. She was admitted into the hospital and stayed for 3 Days.

My son was back in the custody of the state and, had to be hospitalized again. The CPS took custody back of my son. Even though I wasn't involved they put down in court records that I abandoned my son. I got paperwork and everything was in there. Everything the Police report, the alcohol results of my son, the whole story and it also stated at the end of this that the state is willing to give custody back to Jack if he went to some meetings and got on meds.

You see, even if he was prescribed meds he'd just throw them away unless they got him high. A quick note my son was sick he needed to be on meds and had been on them when he was with me. Dad never made him take his meds. I could not believe it. Wow, were they serious? They are going to give custody back to Jack?

First thing I did was contact the officer that took Jack to the hospital that night and told him about the alcohol level in my sons blood and asked why wasn't Jack charged with giving a minor alcohol? He said, "Dad said he stole it and was sneaking it in his room." And I told him Jack stabbed himself and blamed the child for it. He said he would check it out and get back to me. I Never heard back.

Jack got 2 years for the assault on his mother this was the 5th time in one year he hurt her so they gave him time. To this day I don't believe he's done yet. When he gets out of prison he'll try to contact me.

I've got protection that would never let anyone hurt me. For that I will be forever be thankful. My son was placed in the states custody when he was asked if he would go live with mom the answer was no. So as you can see, many times I have tried to get help for me and my son but, the law didn't help at any time.

I have been trying to move on and I admit it is so hard. I miss my little boy more than words can say but I will say this. I pray for his safety and hope for the best.

Chapter 34

Shelby finds Happiness

I want to add a positive note. I met a man and he is amazing he treats me like a princess and he cares. No stress, no yelling and no fighting. We work together as a team and we're best friends and have been together for 4 years but, knew each other a few years before. I can't ask for any better than that.

Over the years the stress and hell I went through took a toll on my health; COPD and Fibromyalgia are among the few but, know that I have never been happier in my life. I have decided to make myself happy and you know that was something I never cared about before. But, you know if you can't be happy in life then what's this life for? To this Day I am shunned by several family members for disowning my son but, I put up a wall.

I am almost 50 and I will enjoy life from now on. My goal is to hopefully sell enough copies of this book to help build our little house and enjoy what life I have left with the man who has brightened my life since the day we hooked up. And also get the word out that there are so many situations that women as well as men are abused both mentally and physically every day.

I want you to know today there is so much support just tell someone the Police, friends, relatives. Don't stay a victim your whole life. Get help and get out you dont deserve it no matter what. That was something I had to tell myself so many times.

With the help of friends and my partner in life, I have told my story. Just to get it off my chest helps. I still have nightmares every night even 11 years after the divorce. I take it day by day. Thanks to all for reading my life's story.

Printed in Great Britain
by Amazon